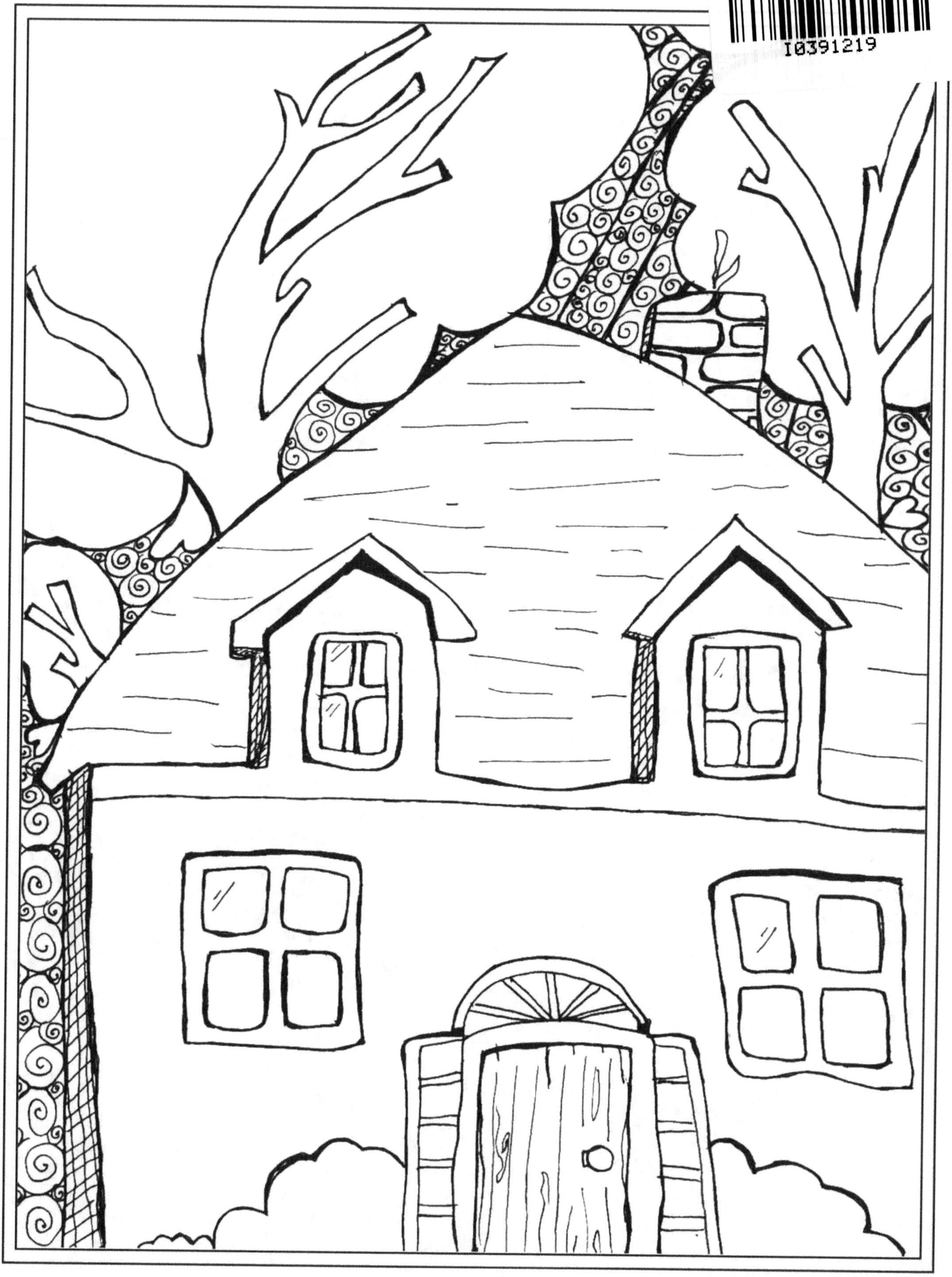

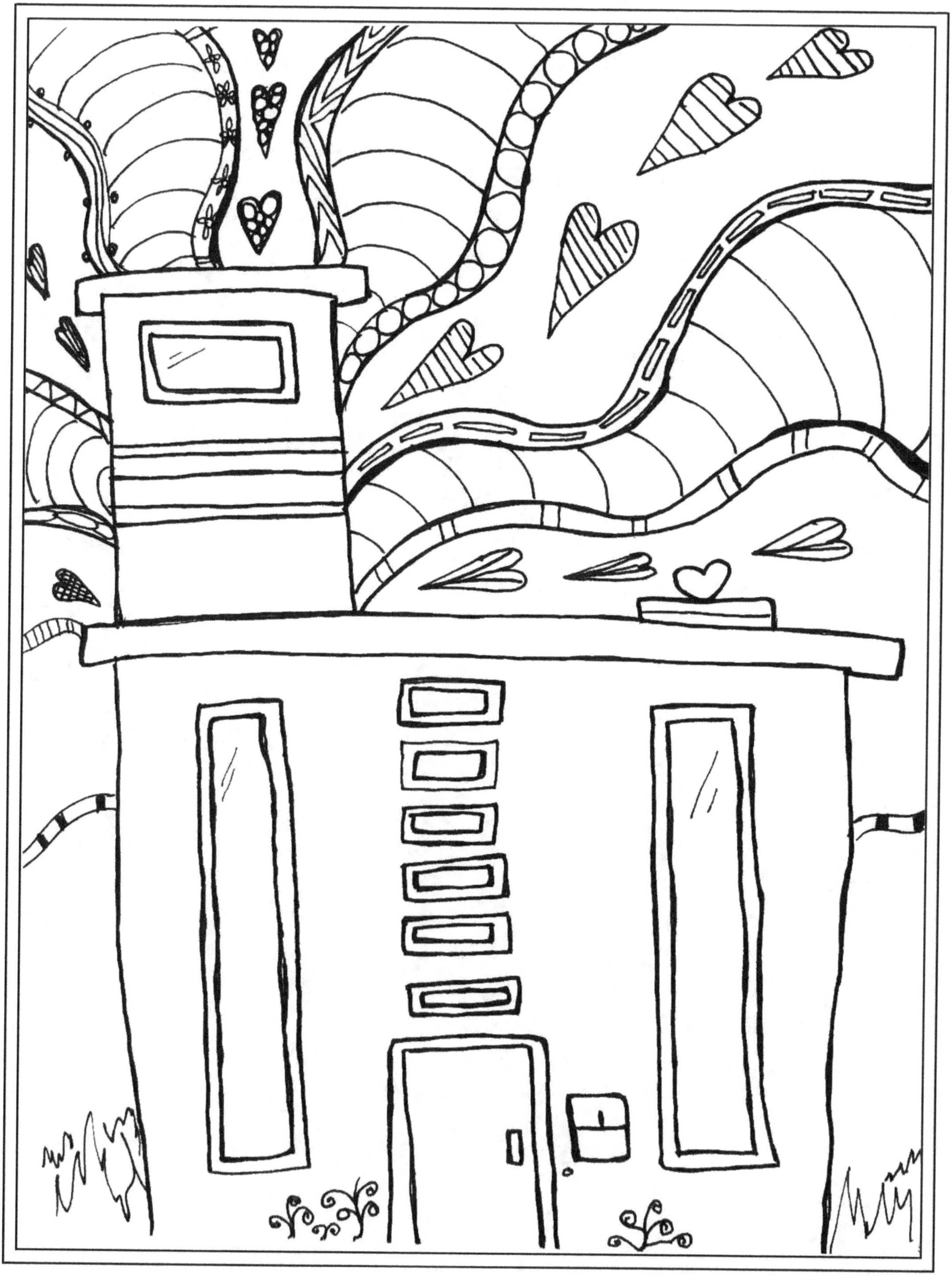

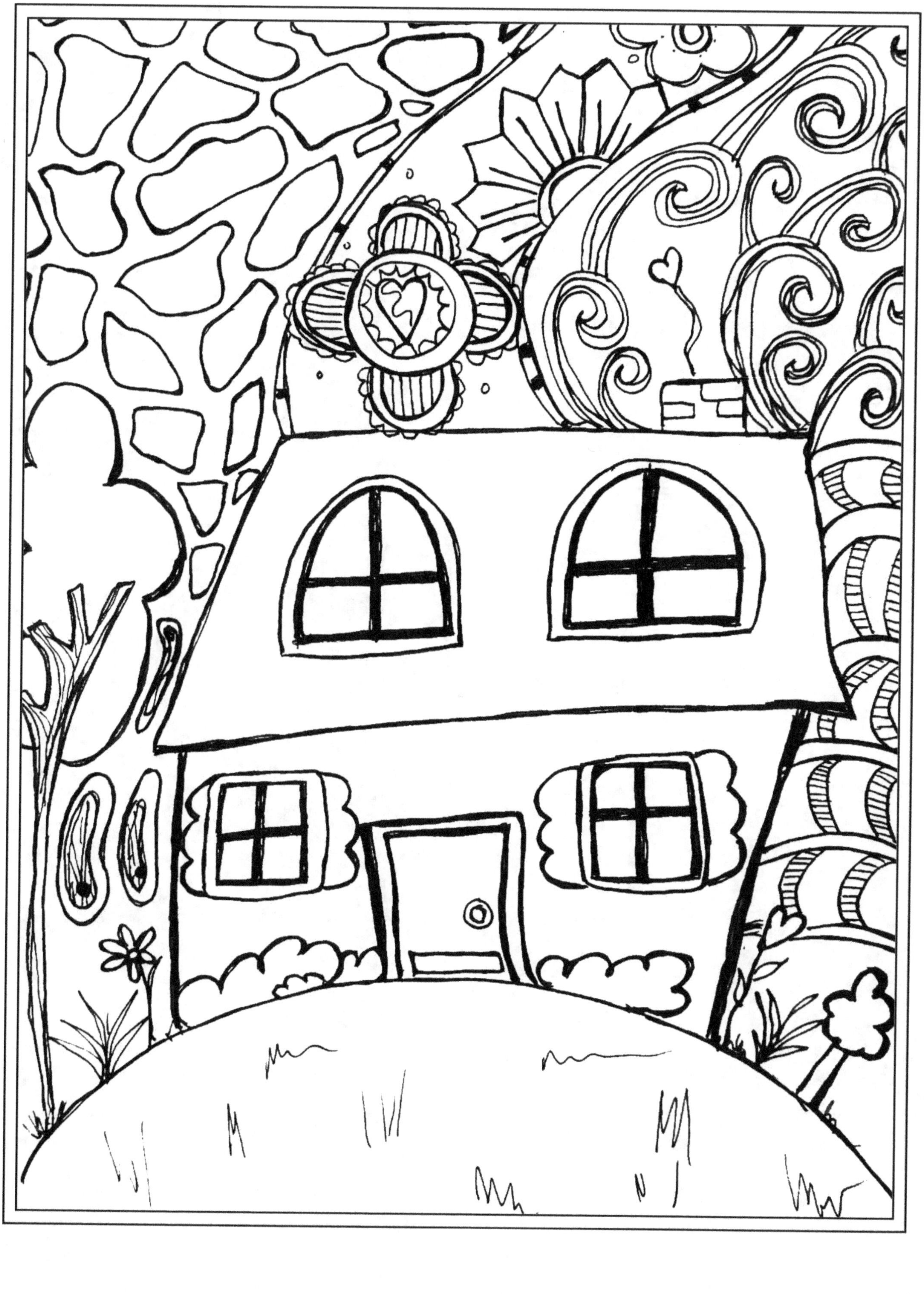

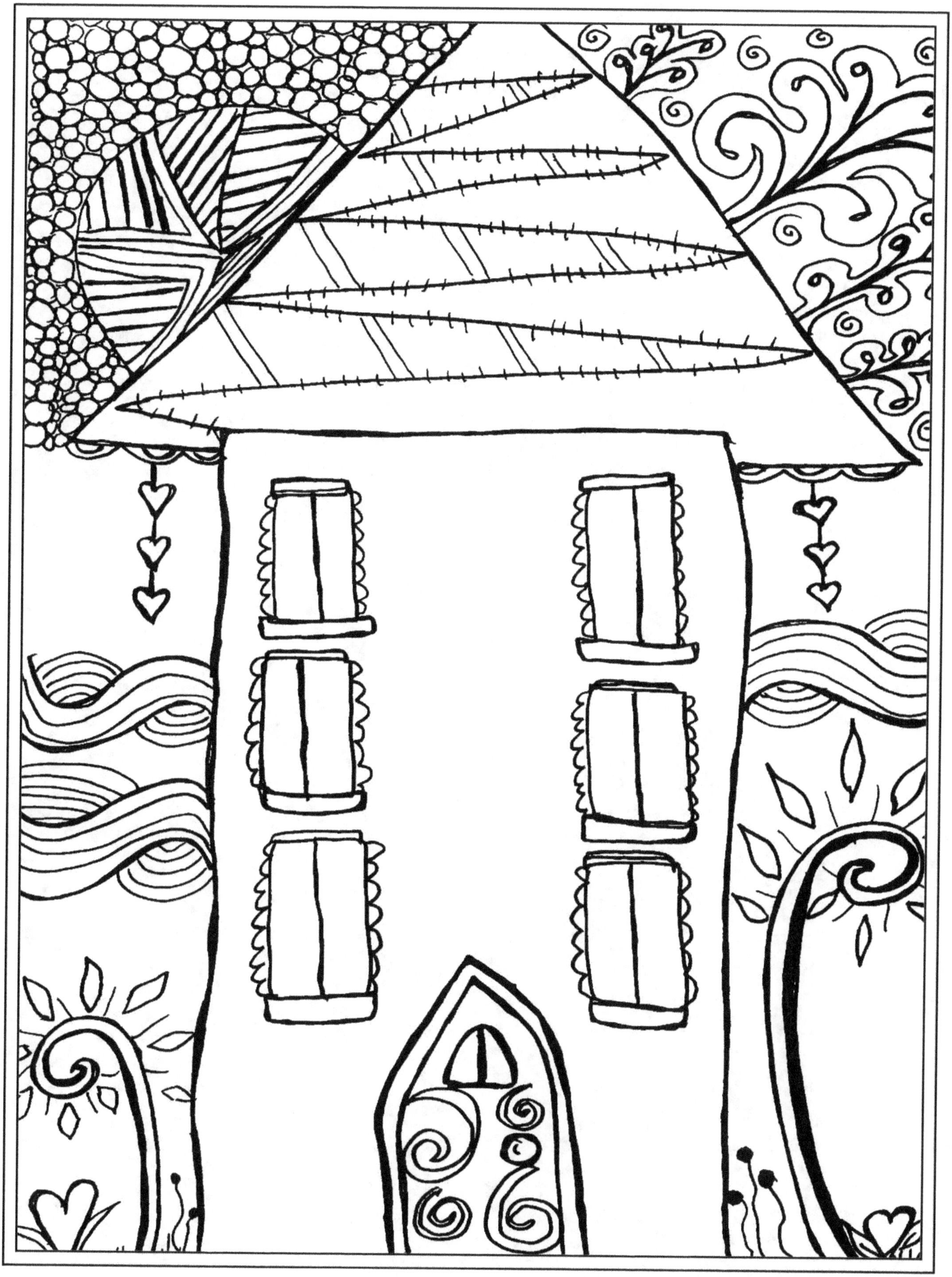

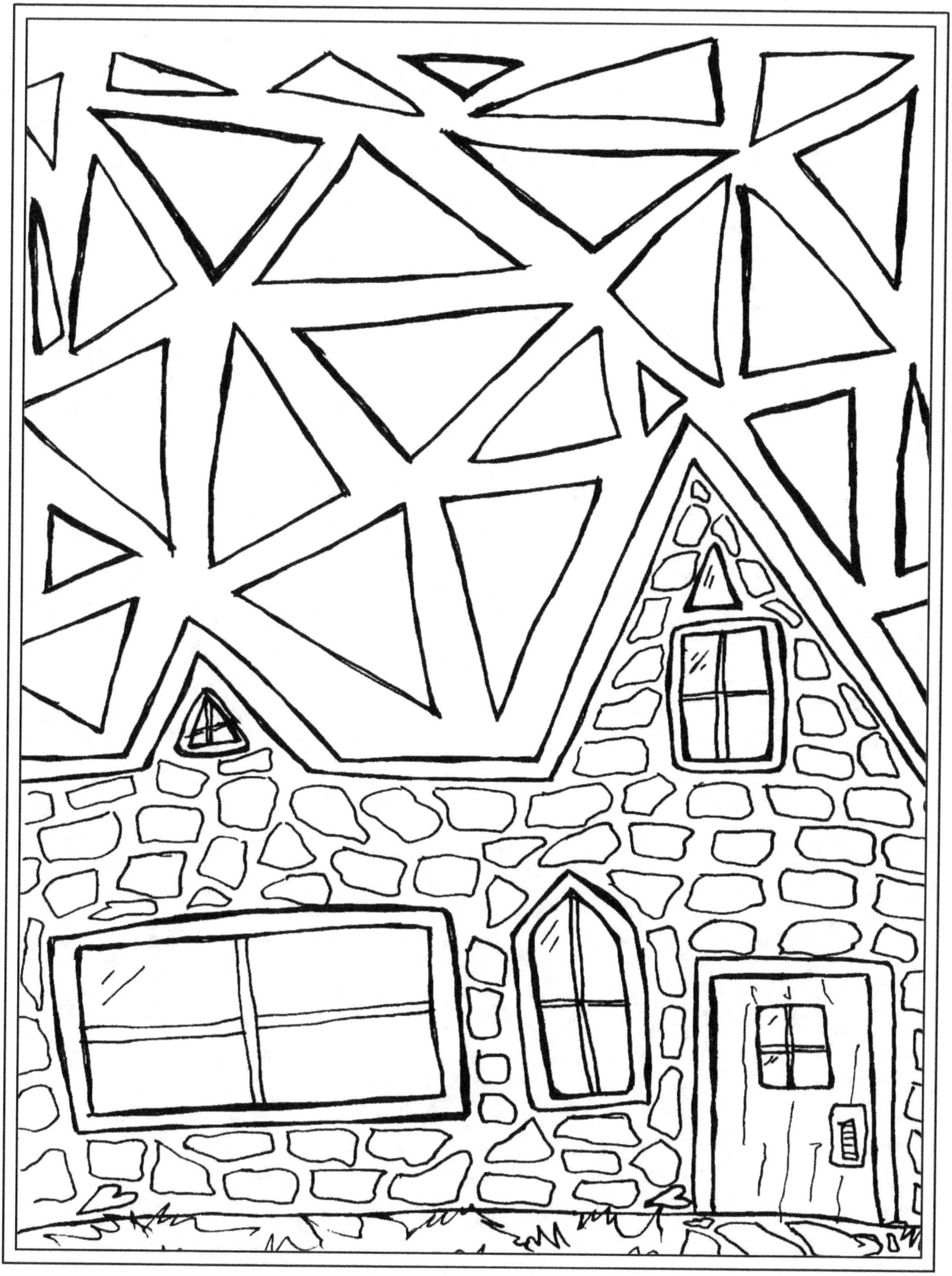

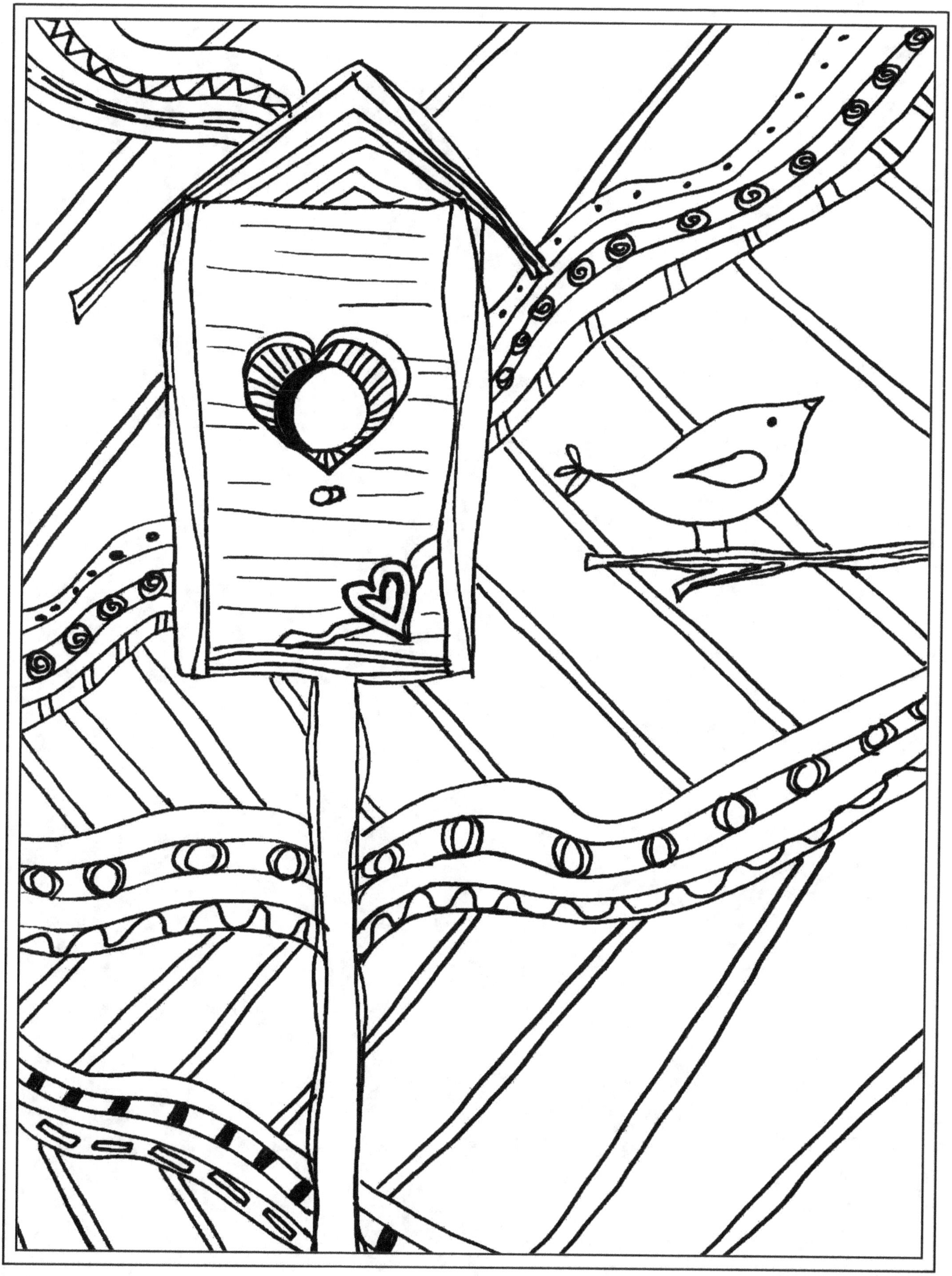

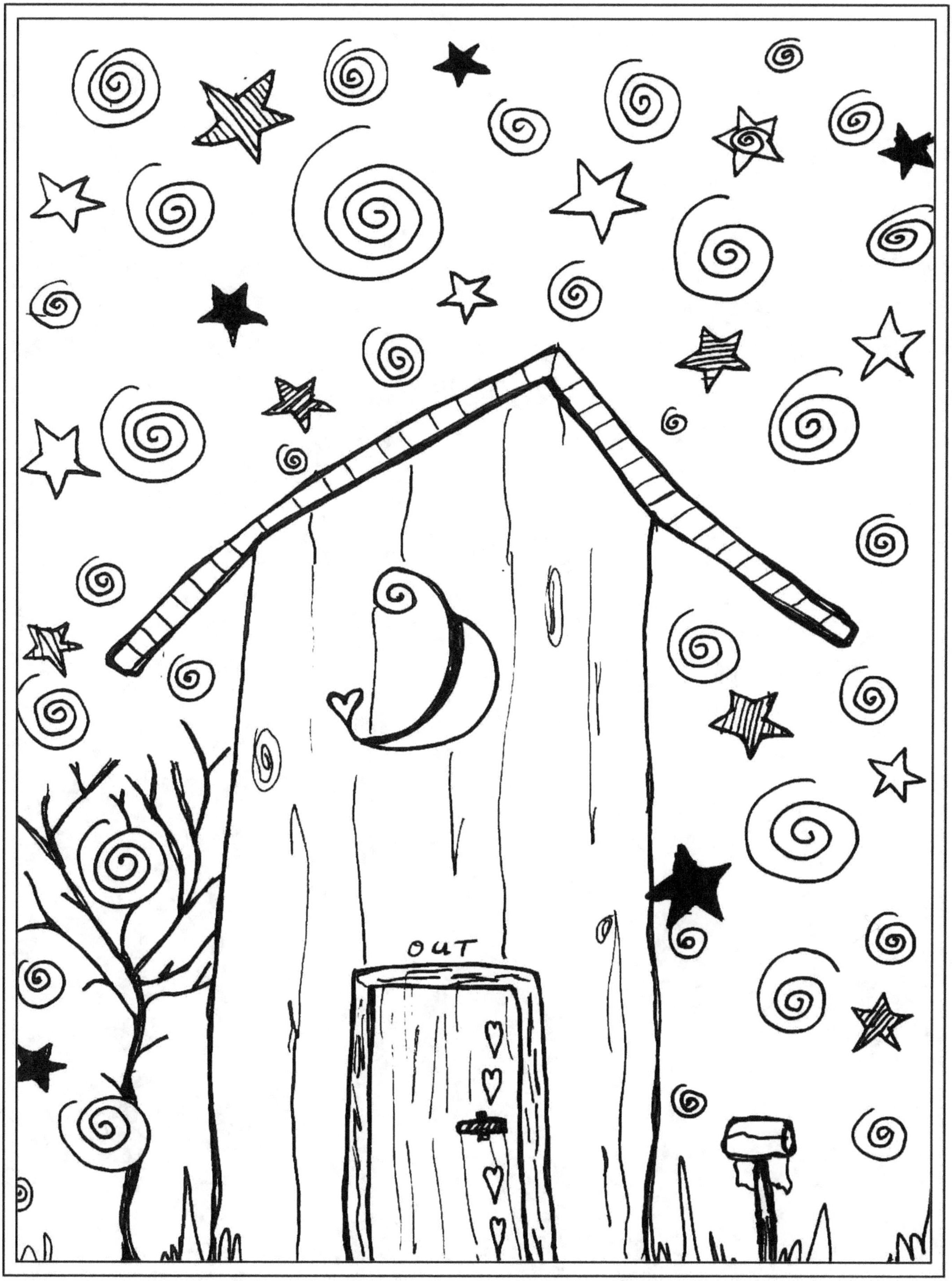
OUT

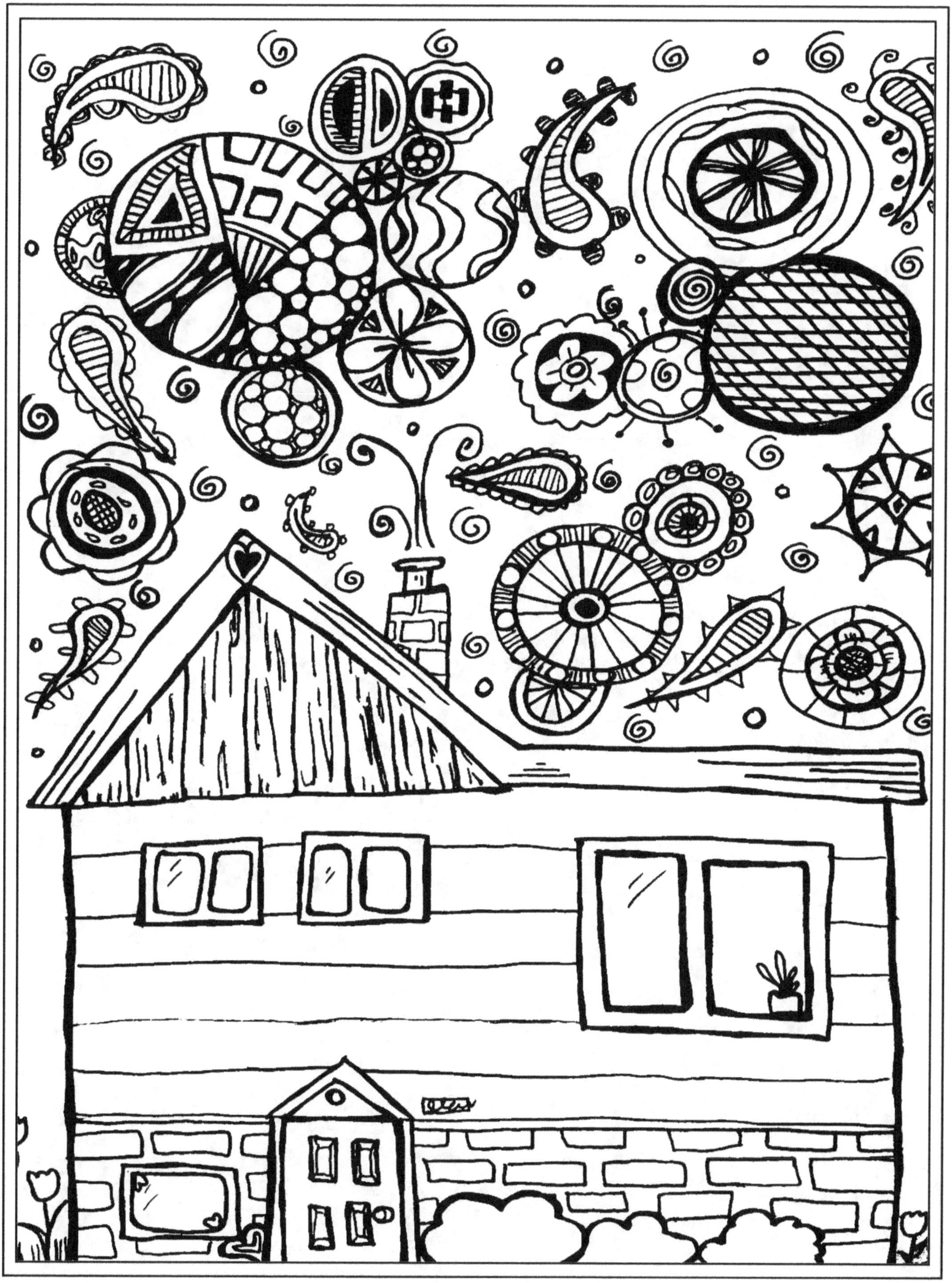

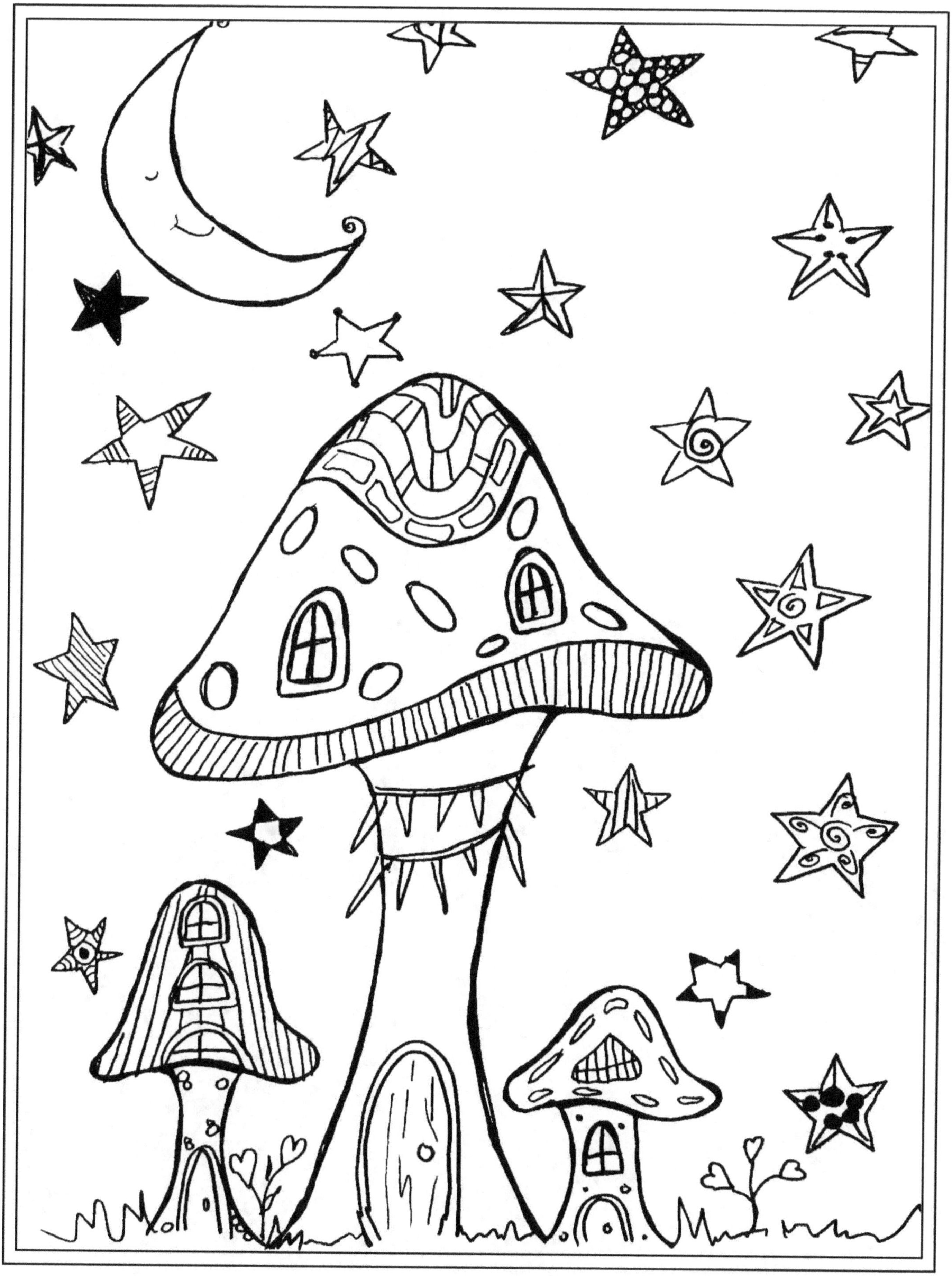

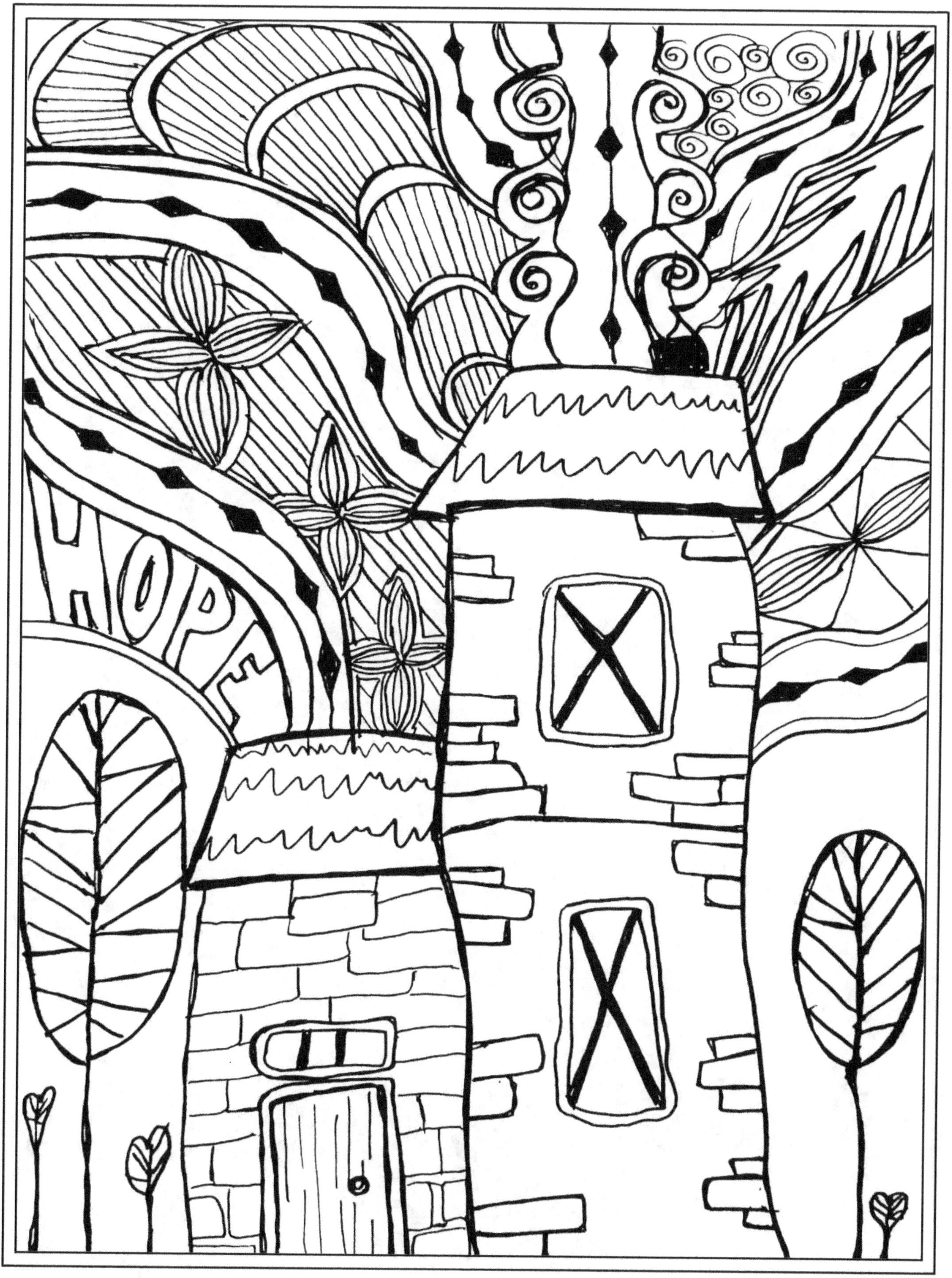
HOPE

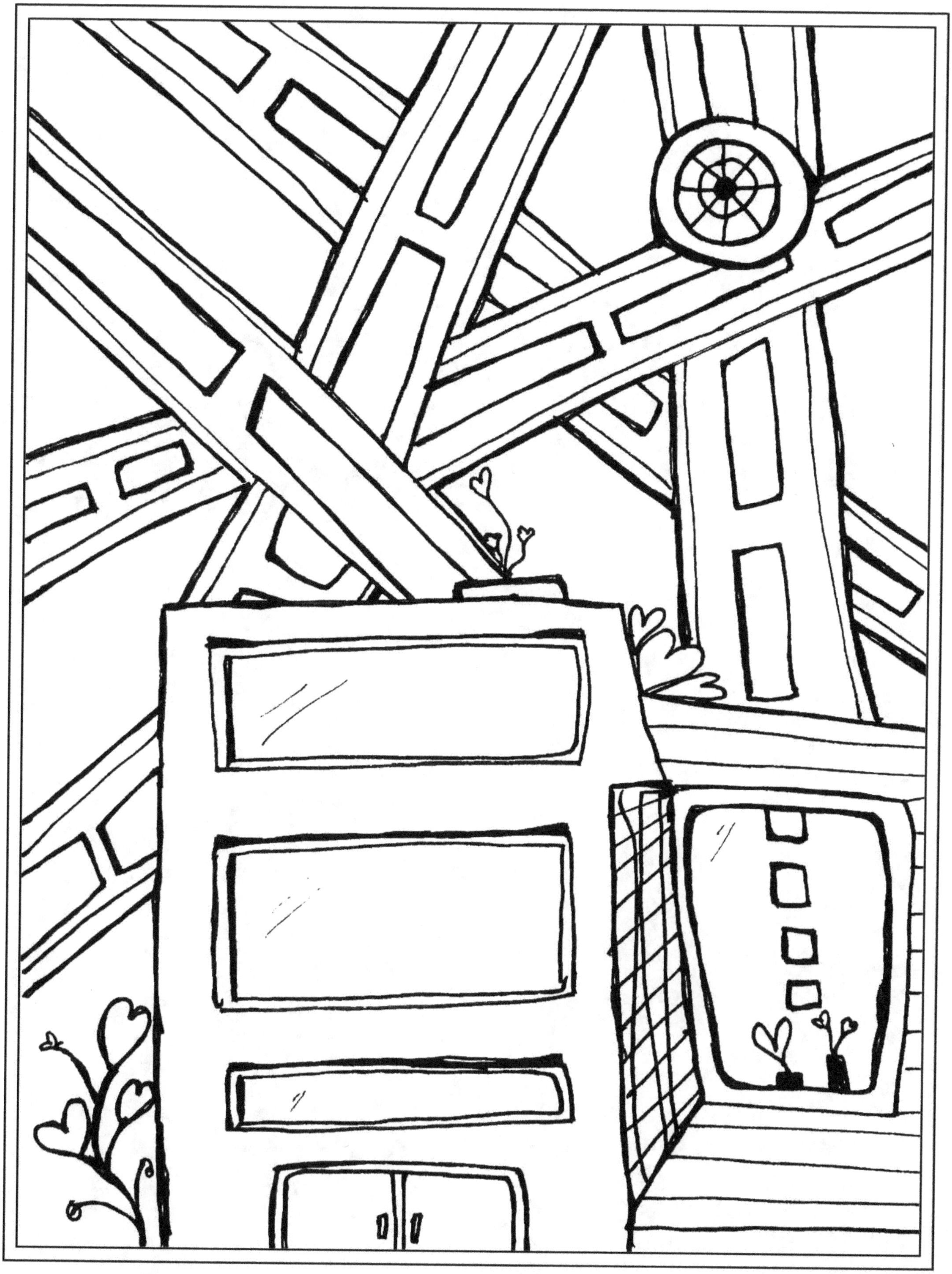

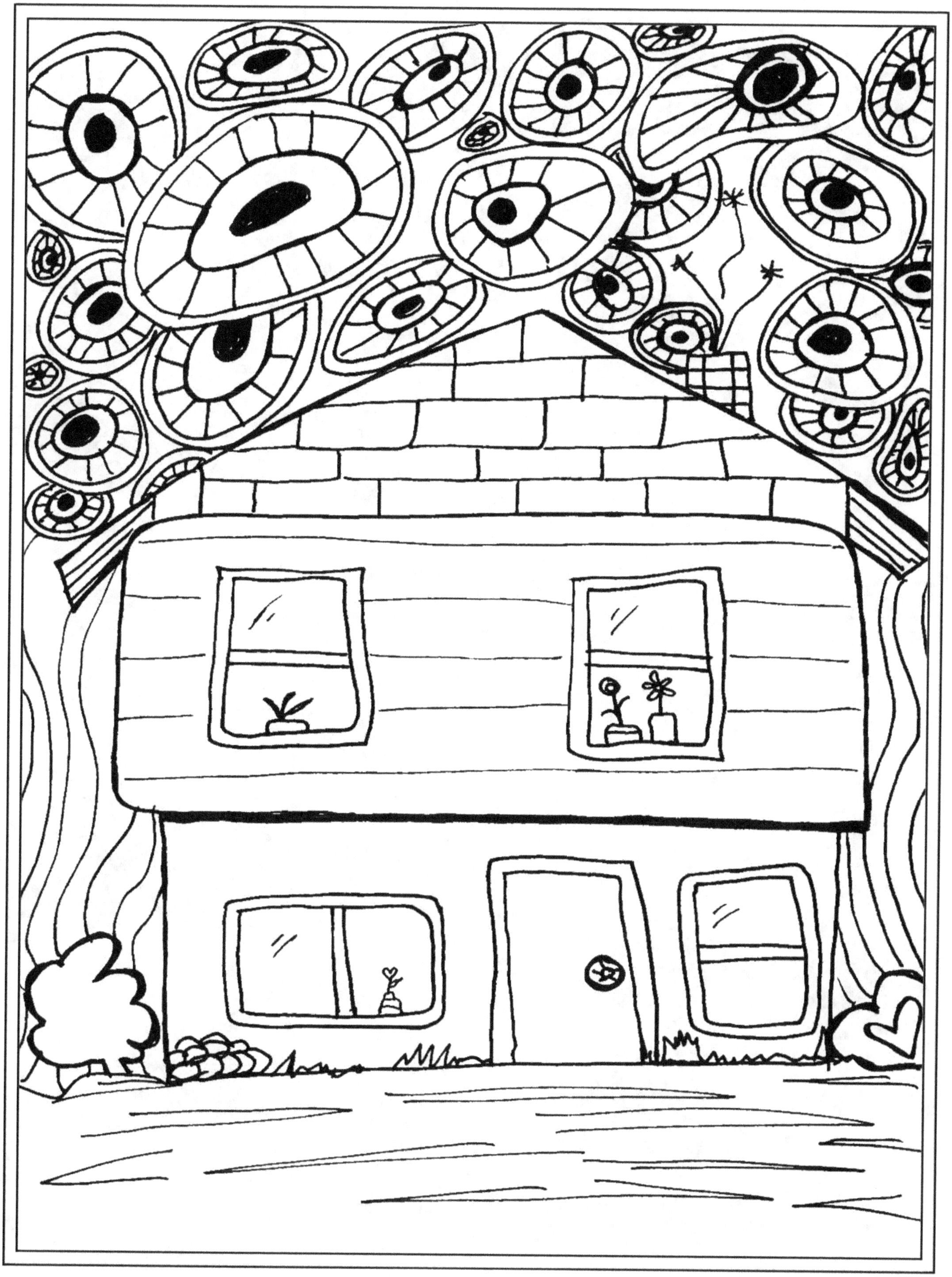

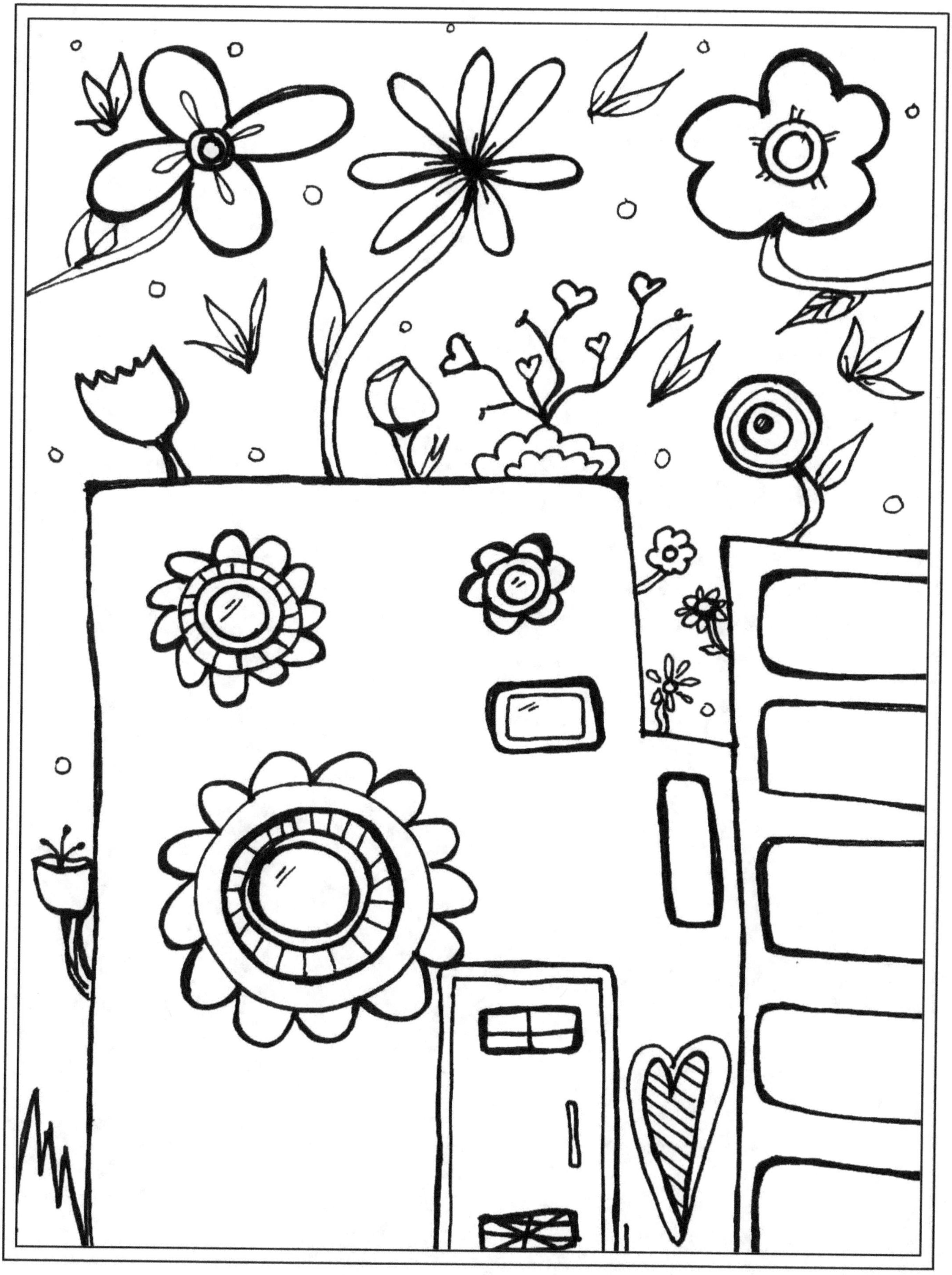

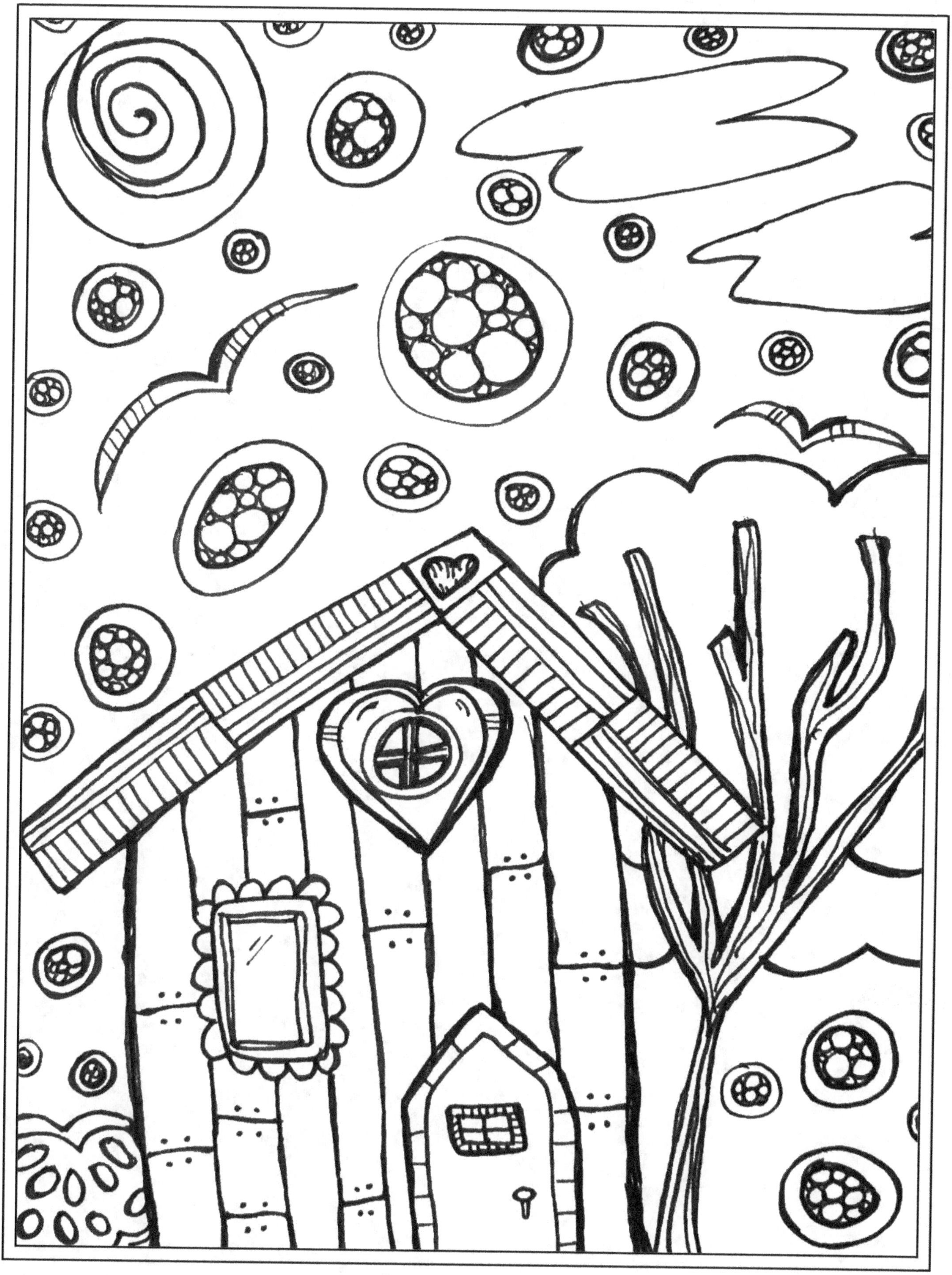

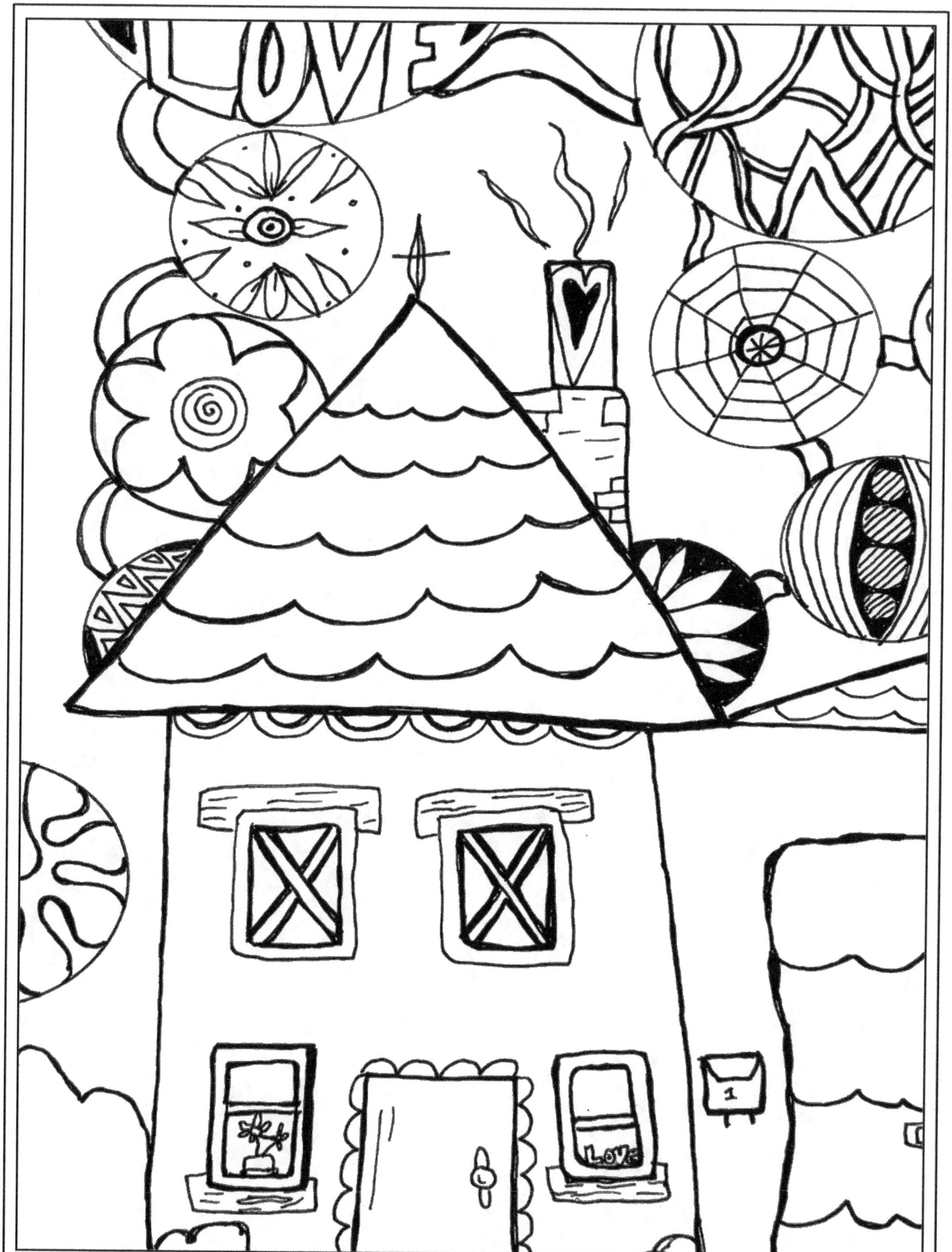
LOVE
1
LOVE

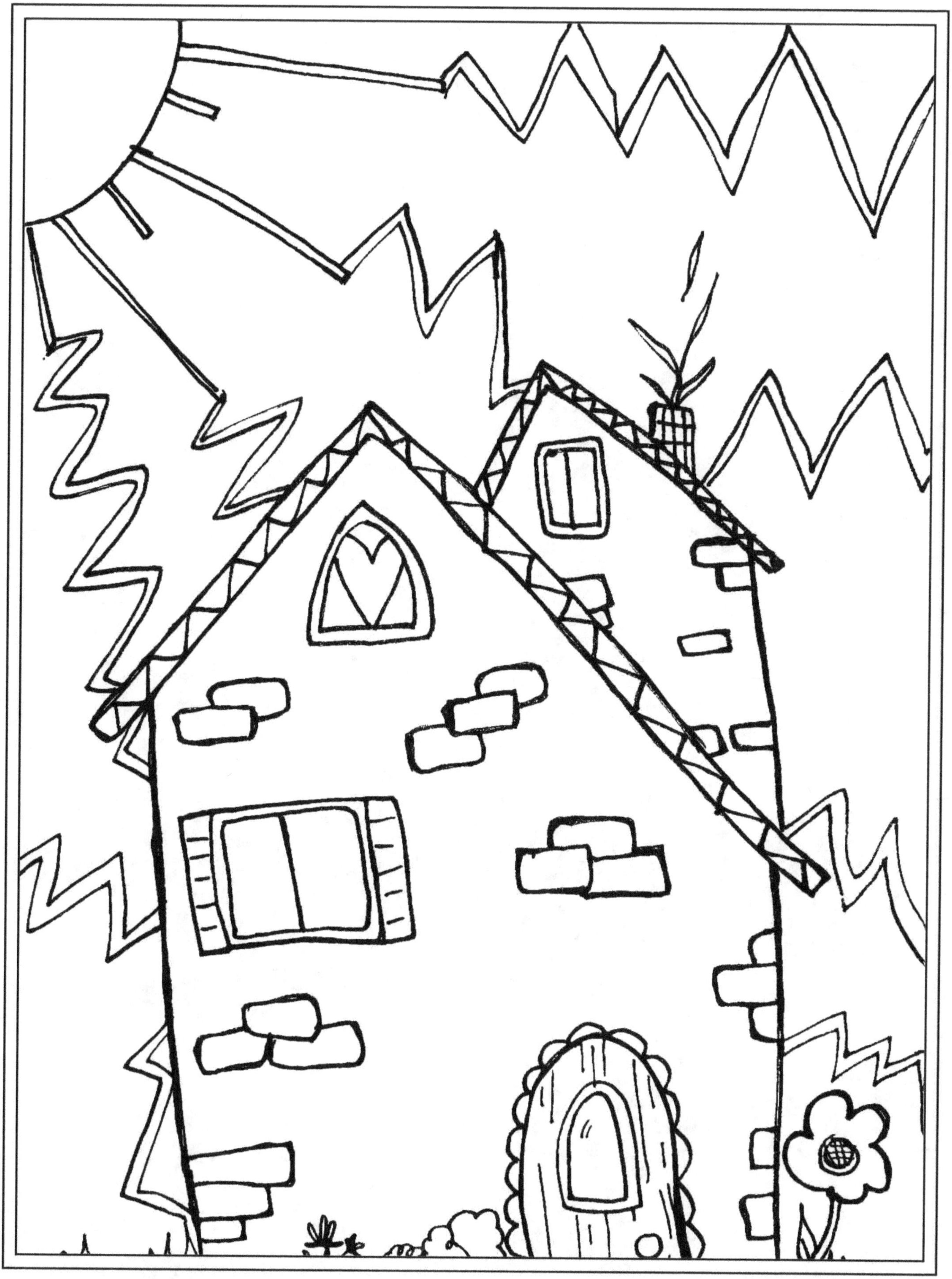

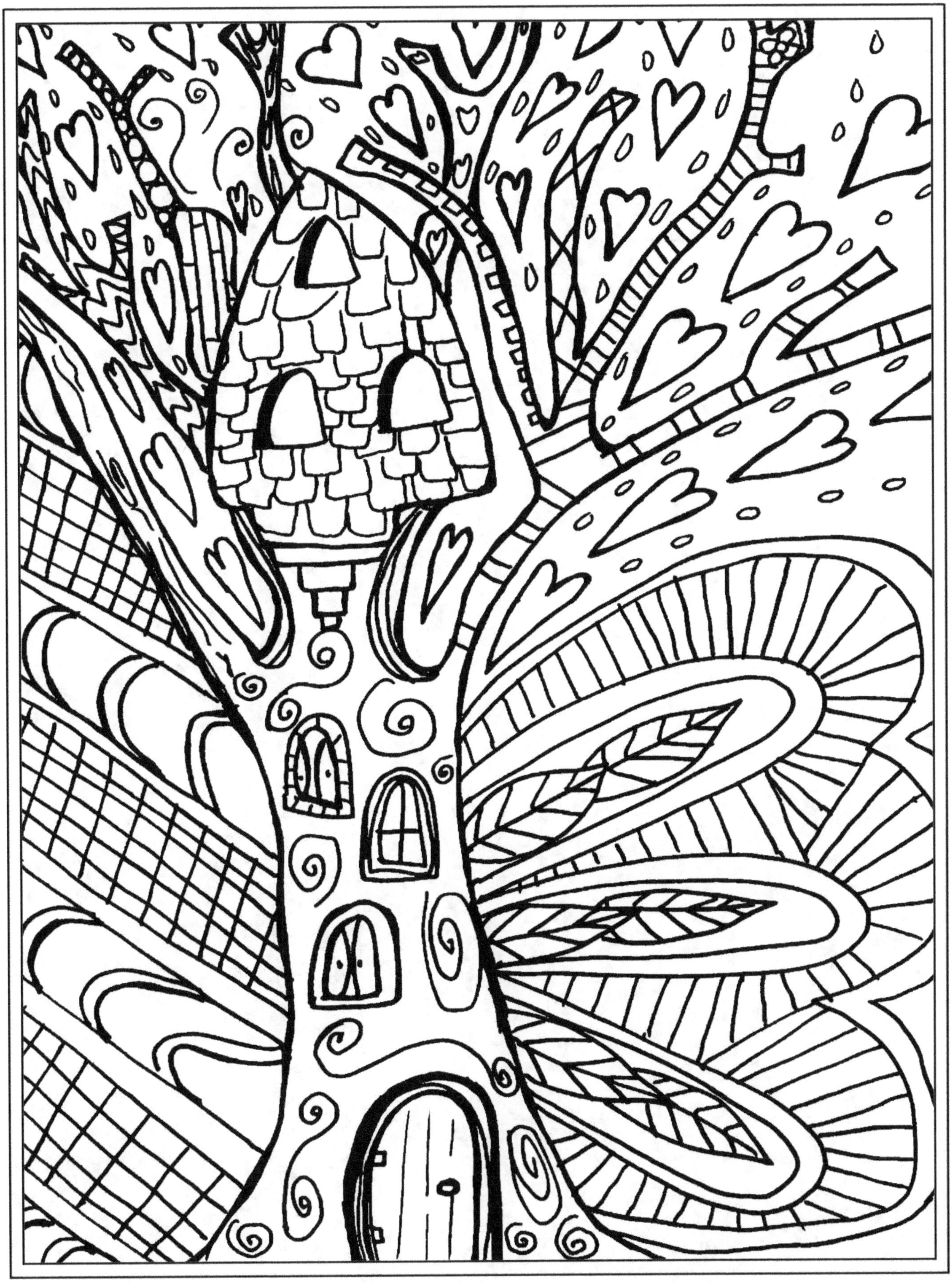

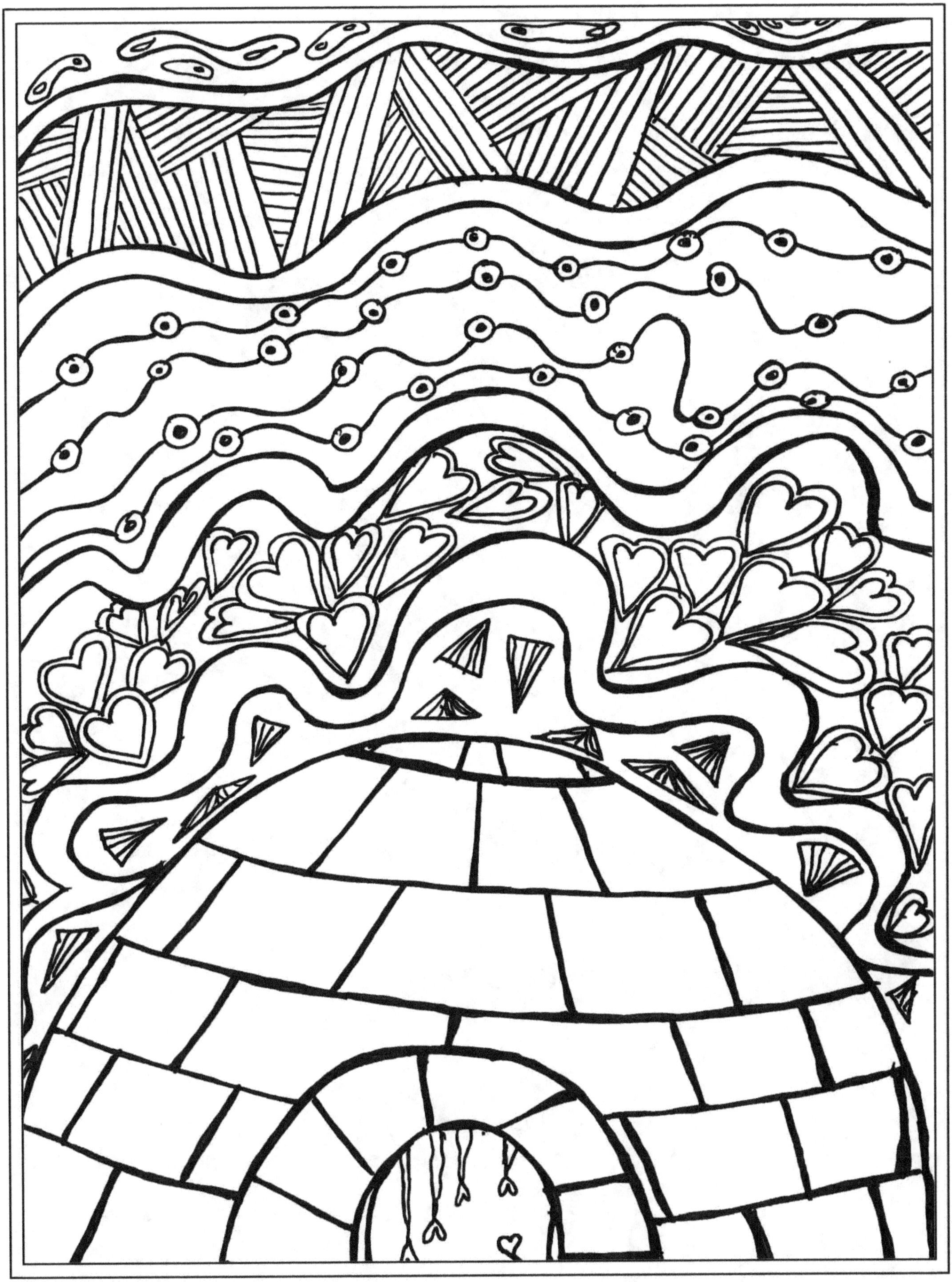

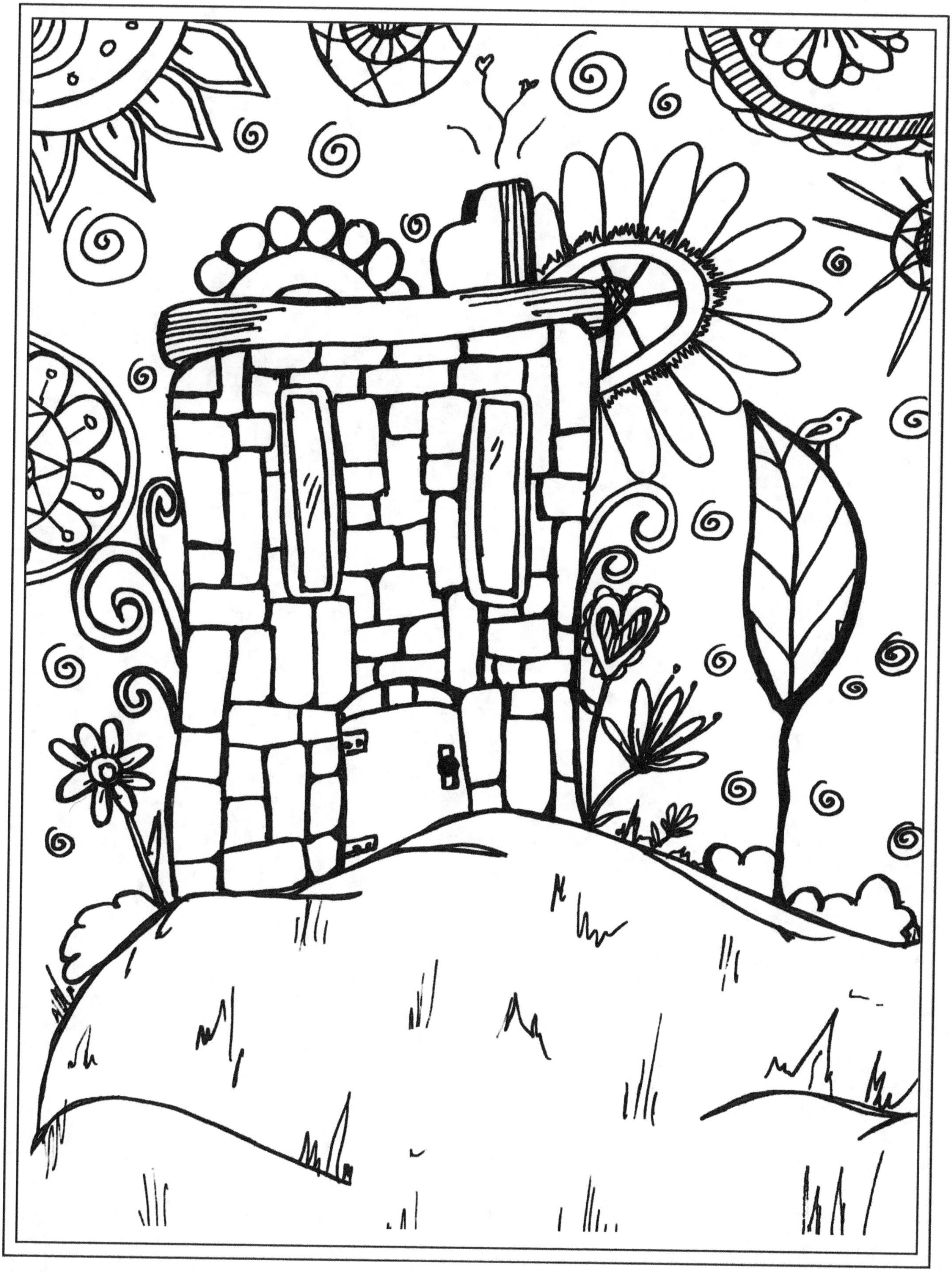

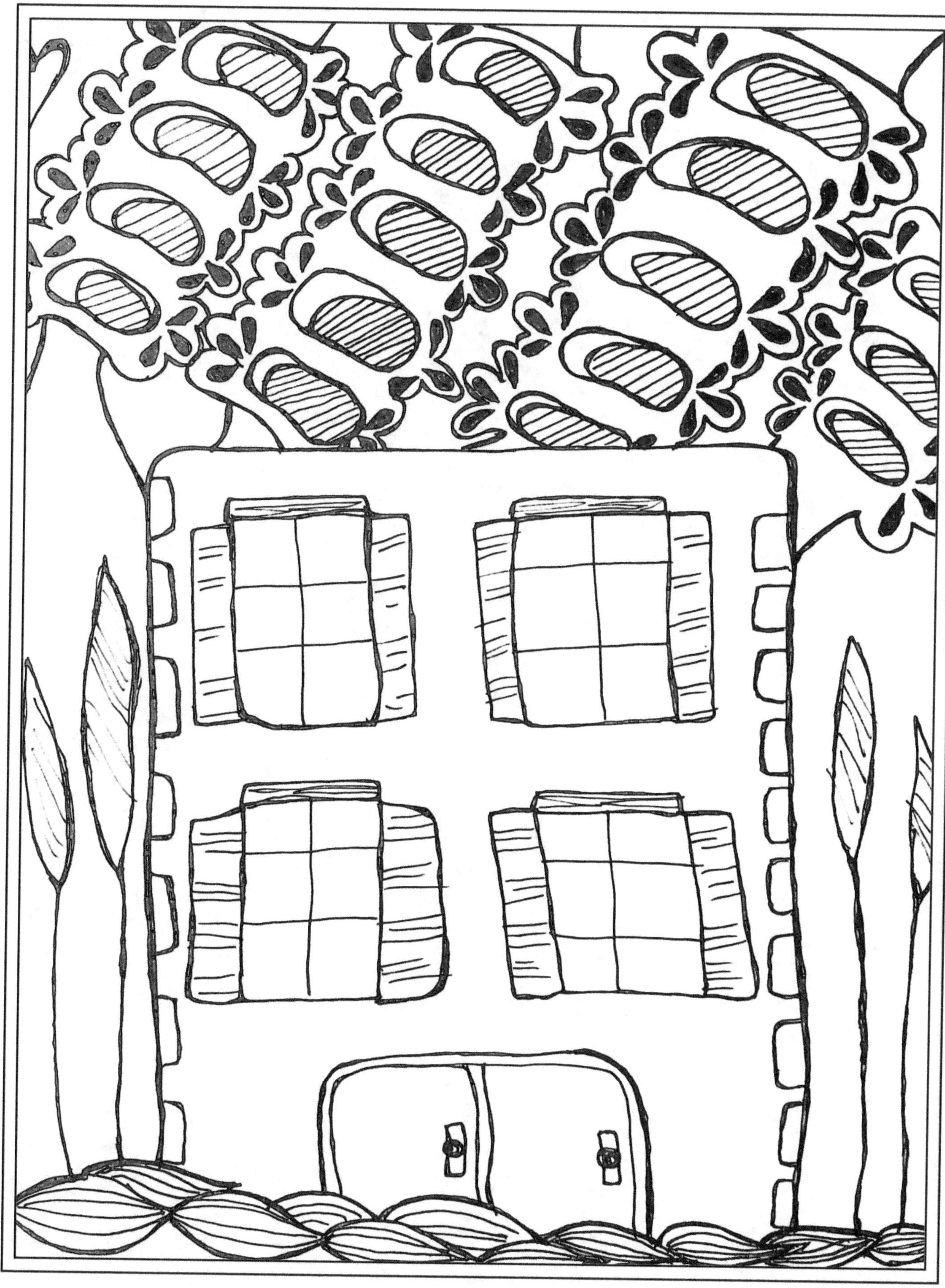

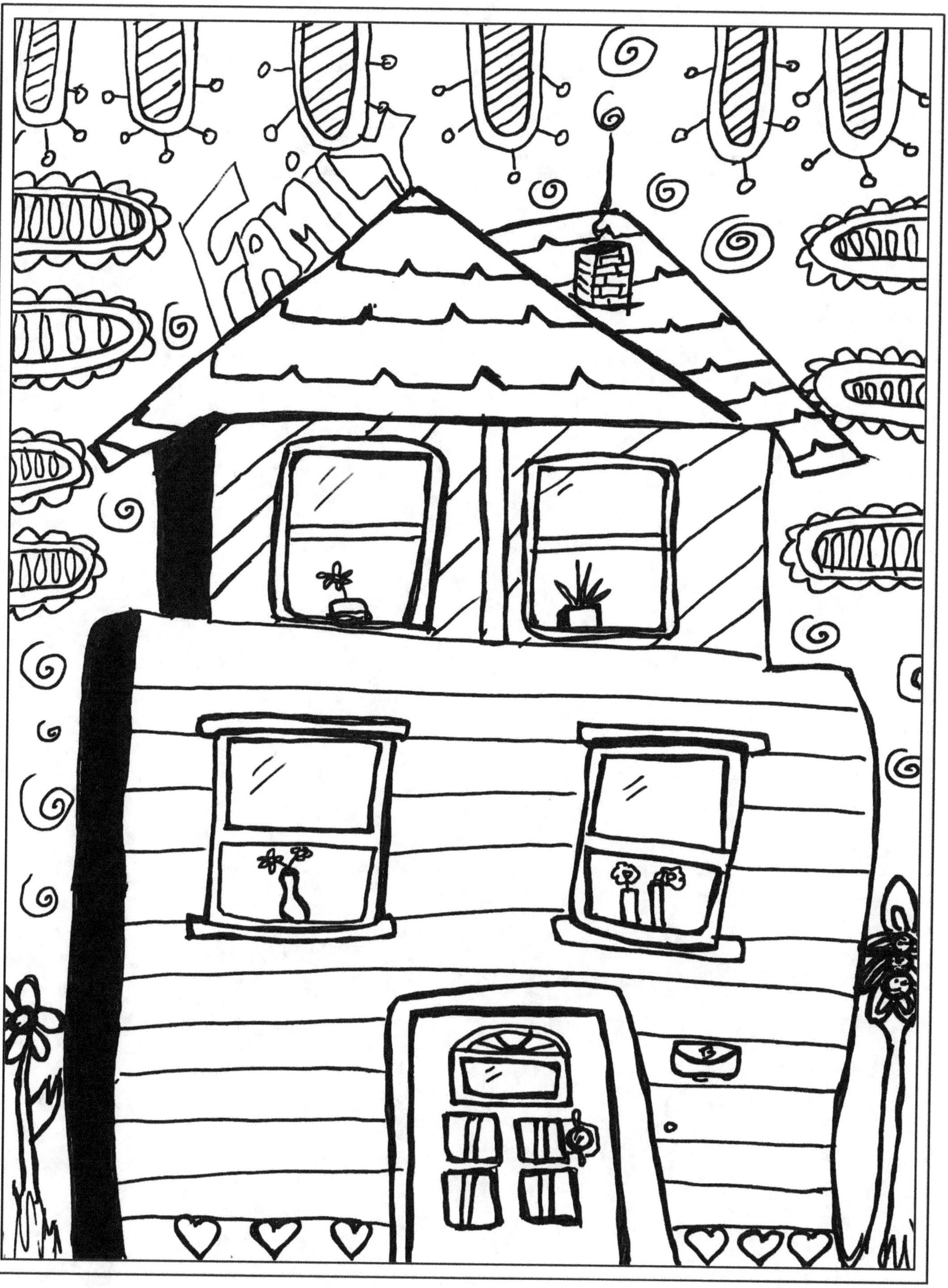

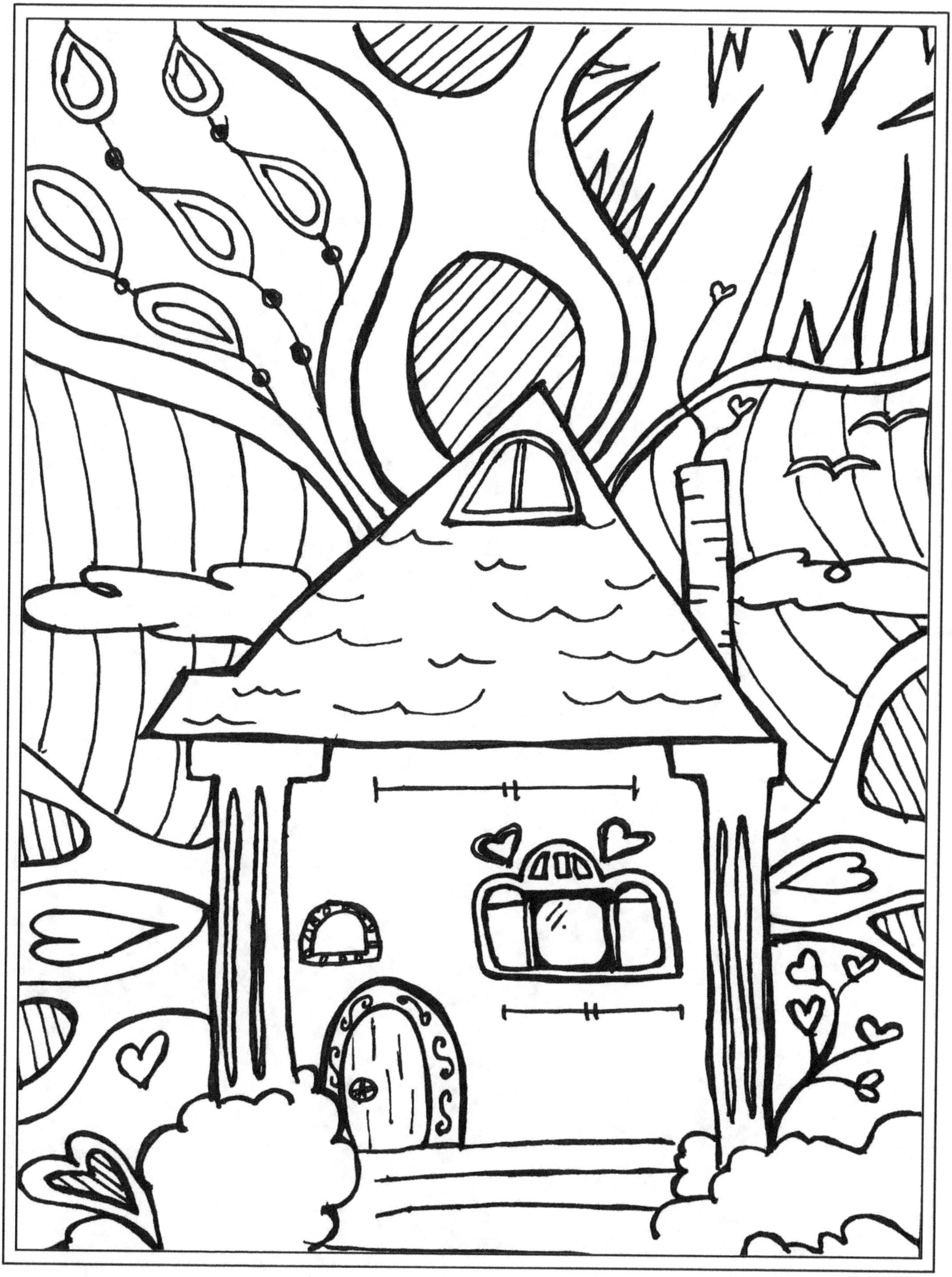

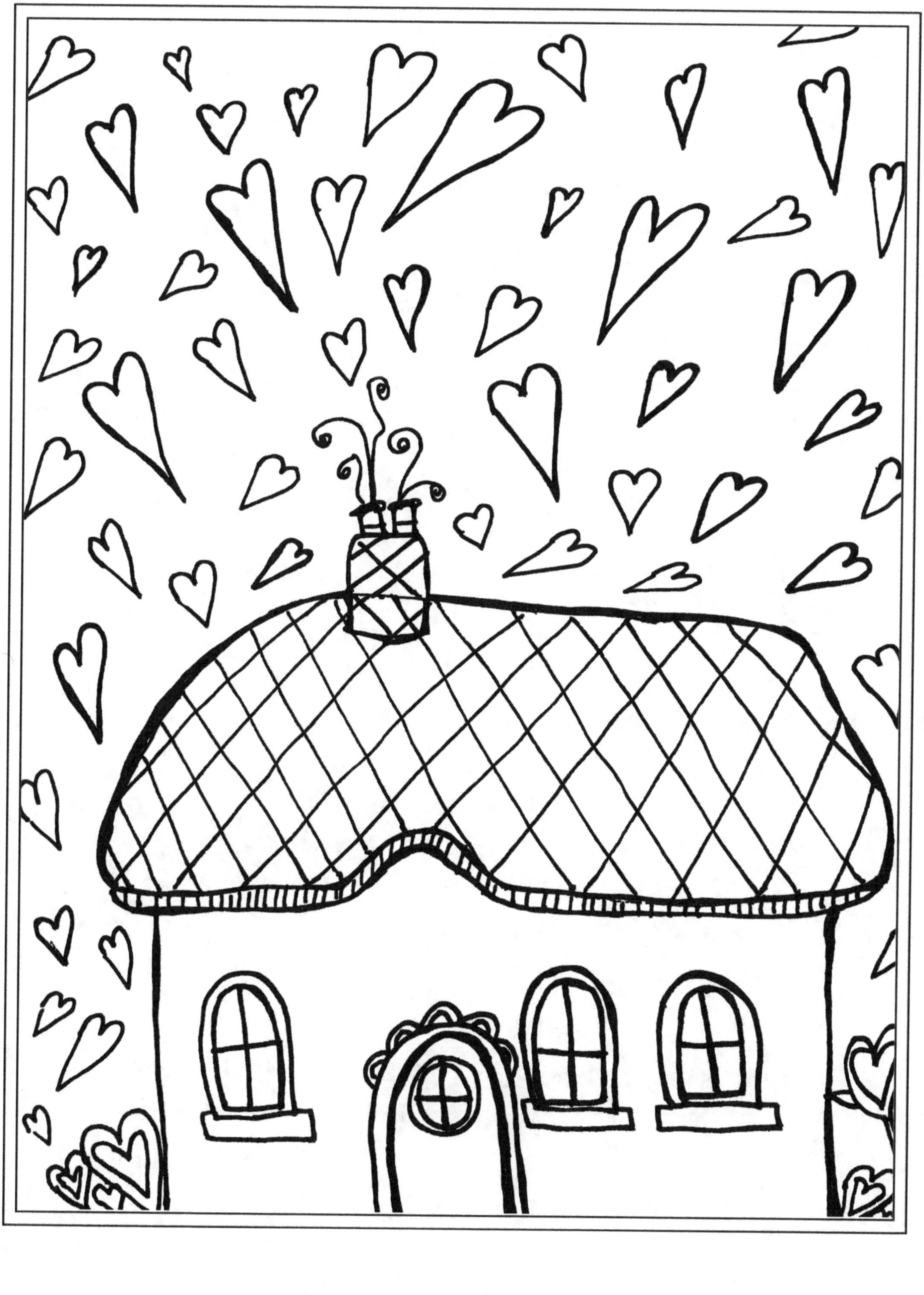

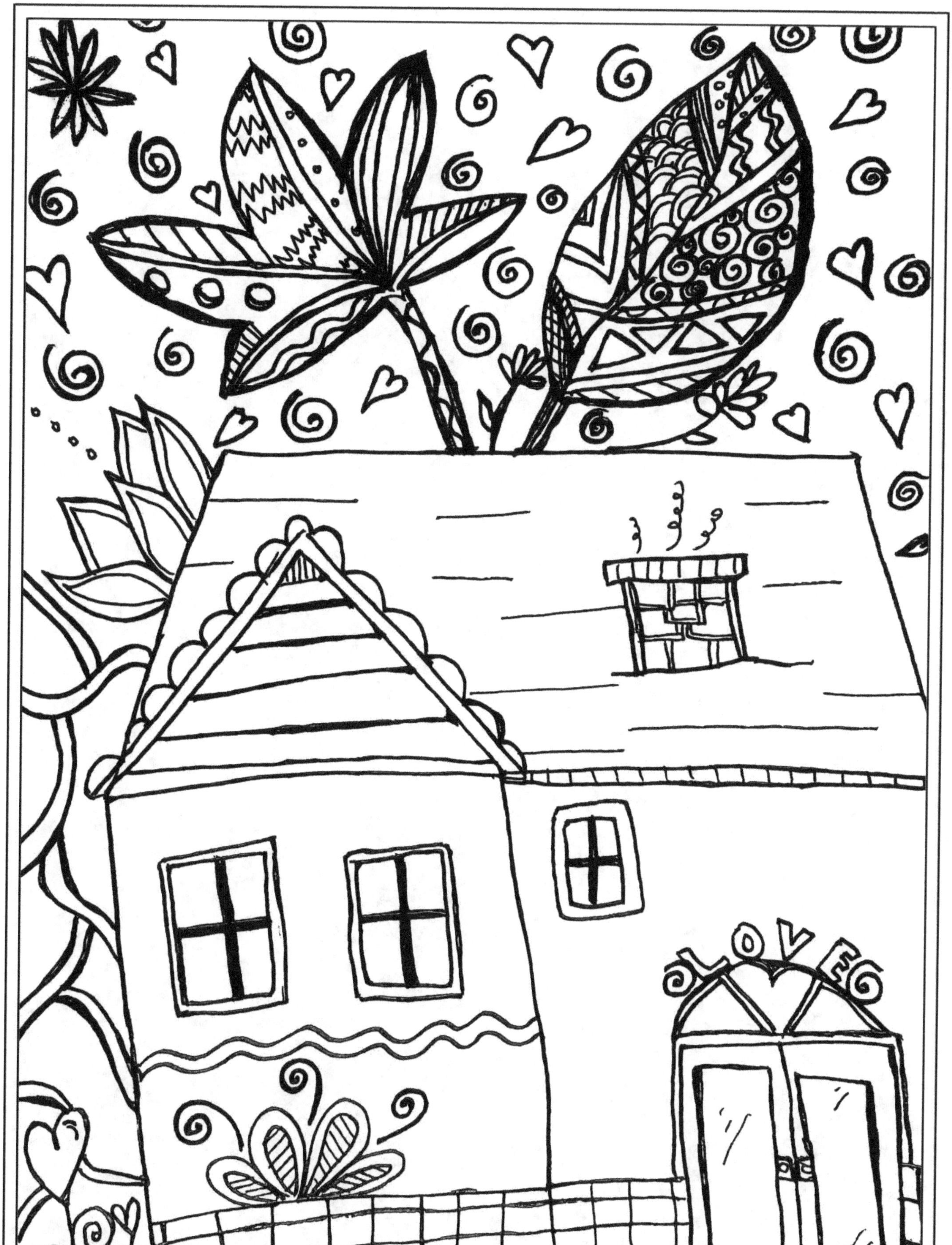
LOVE

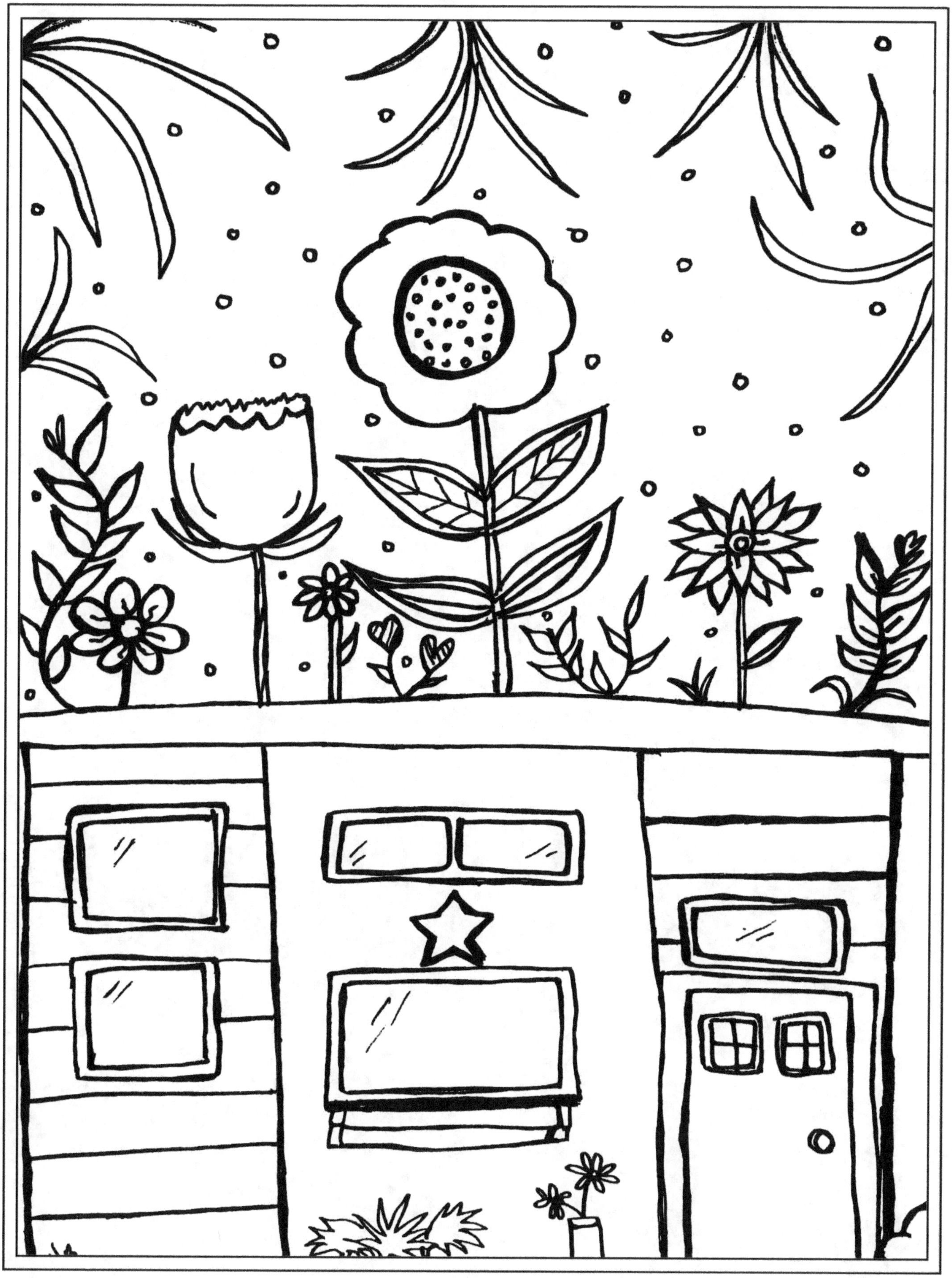

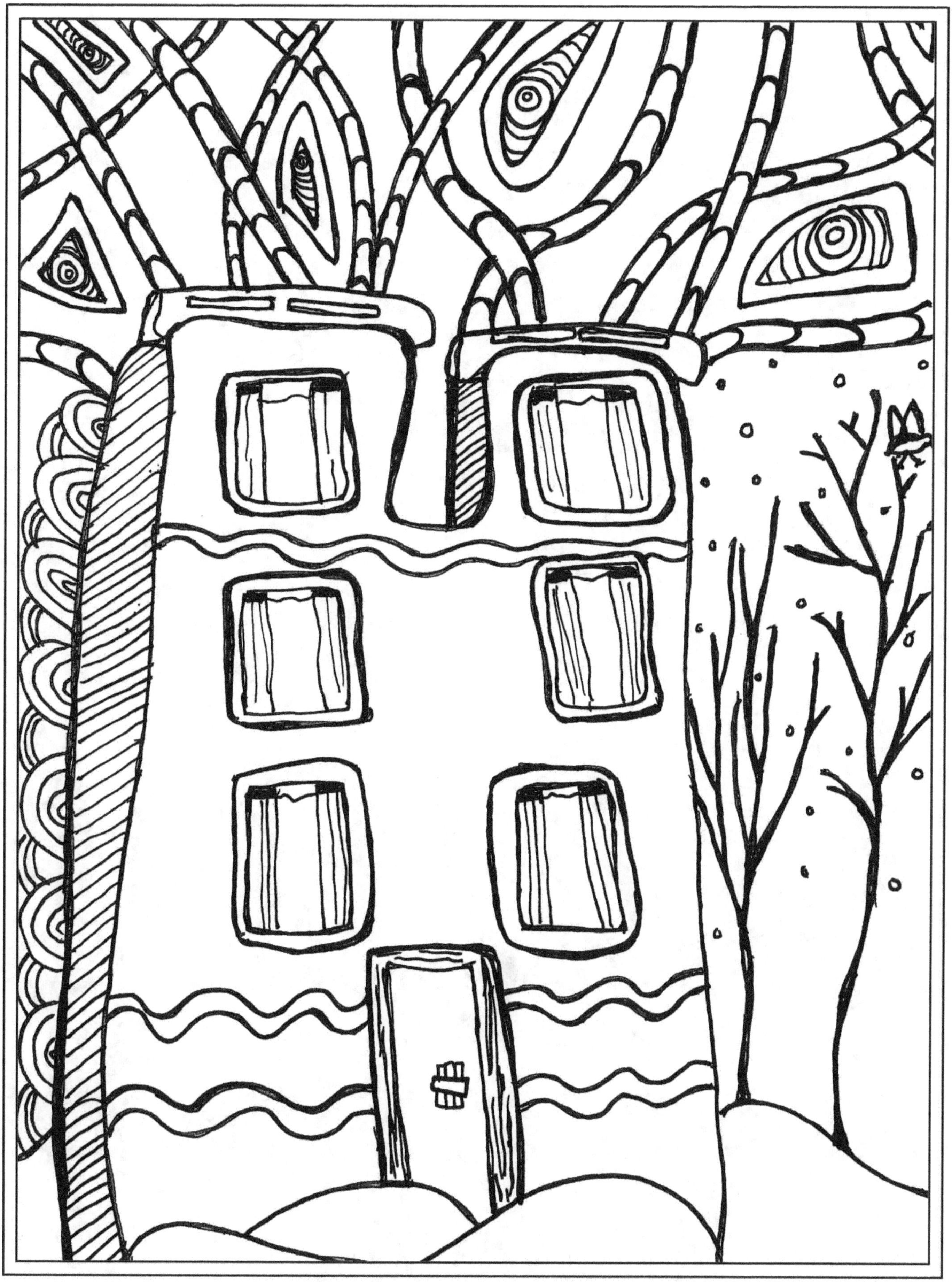

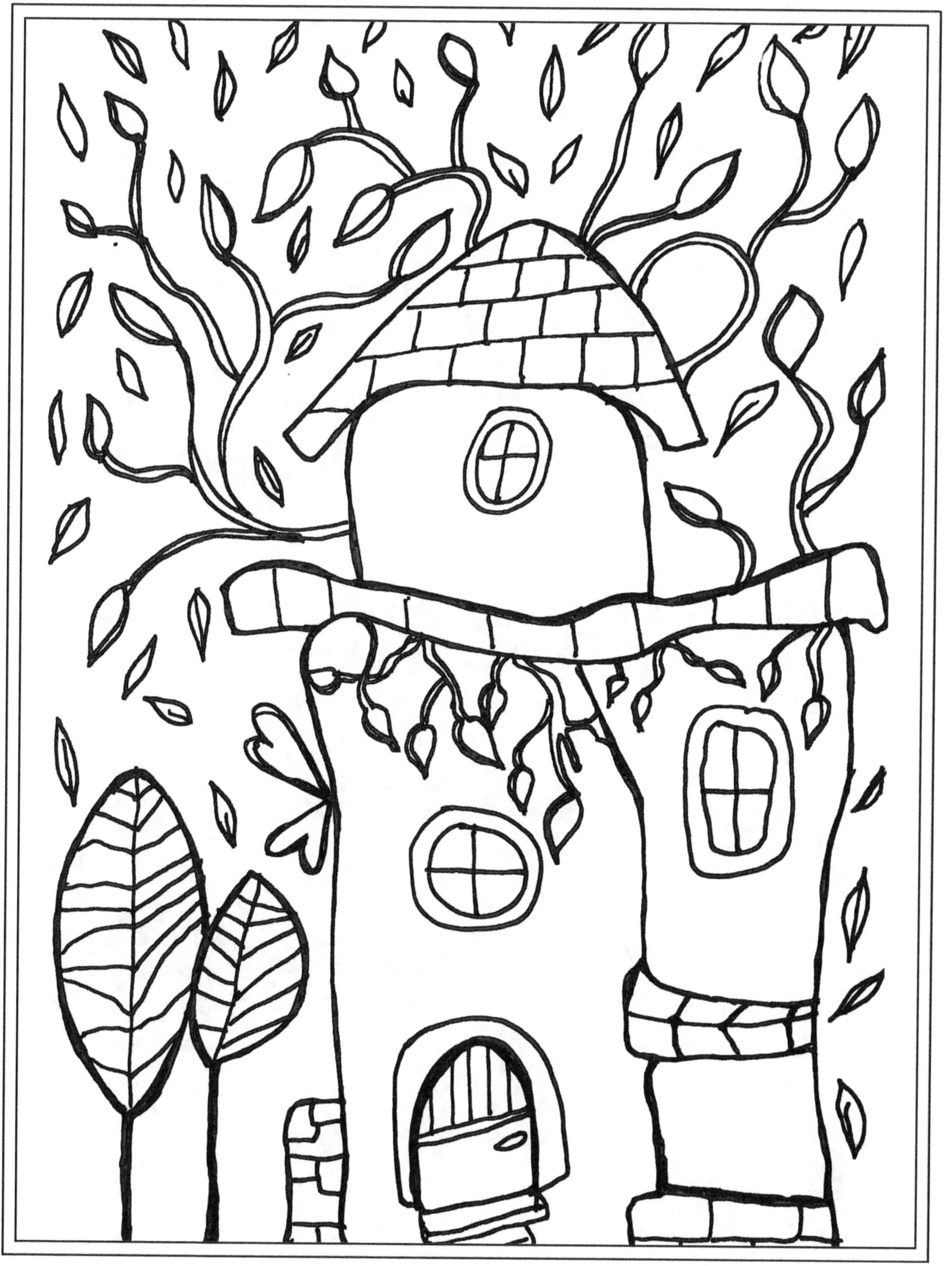

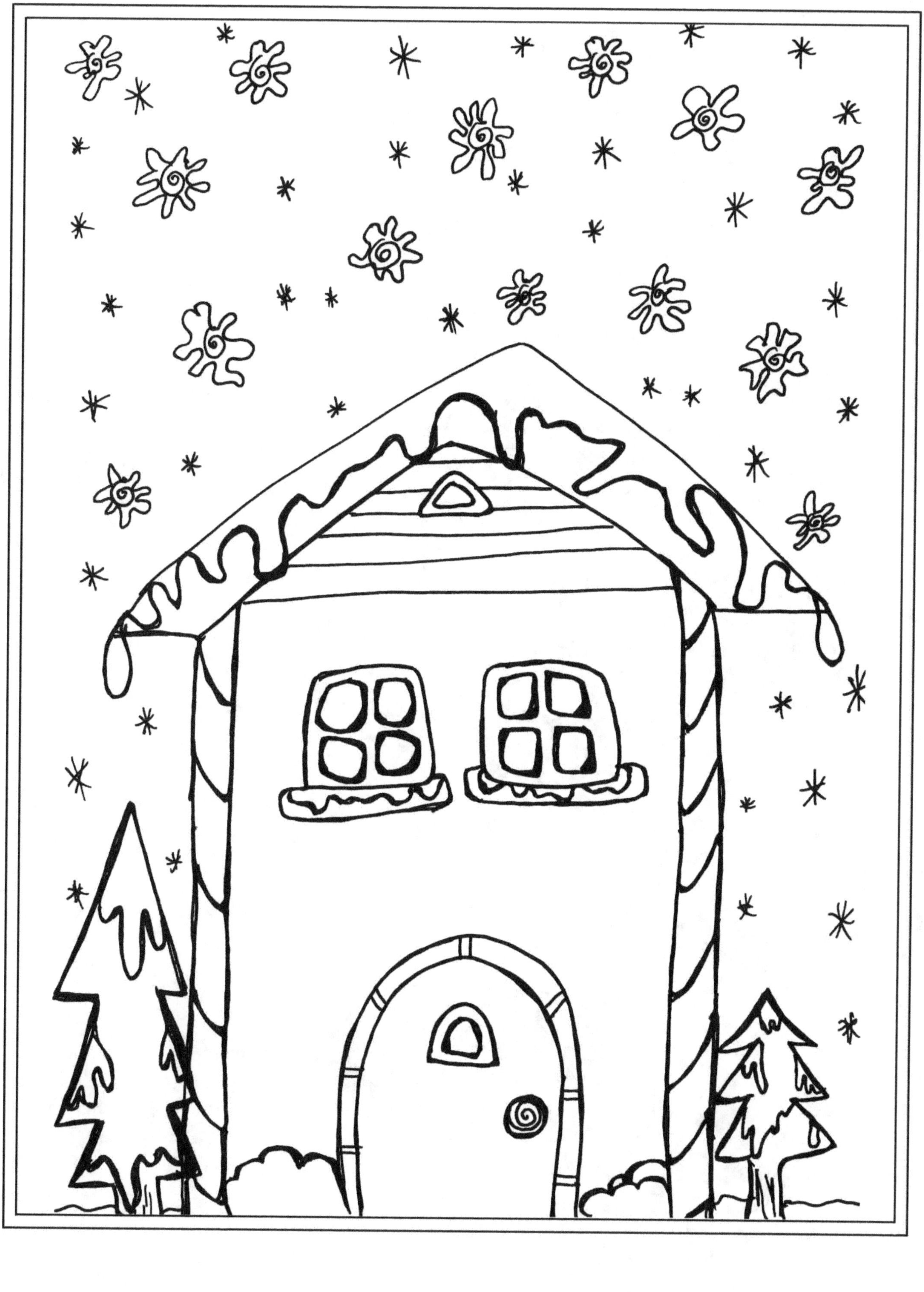

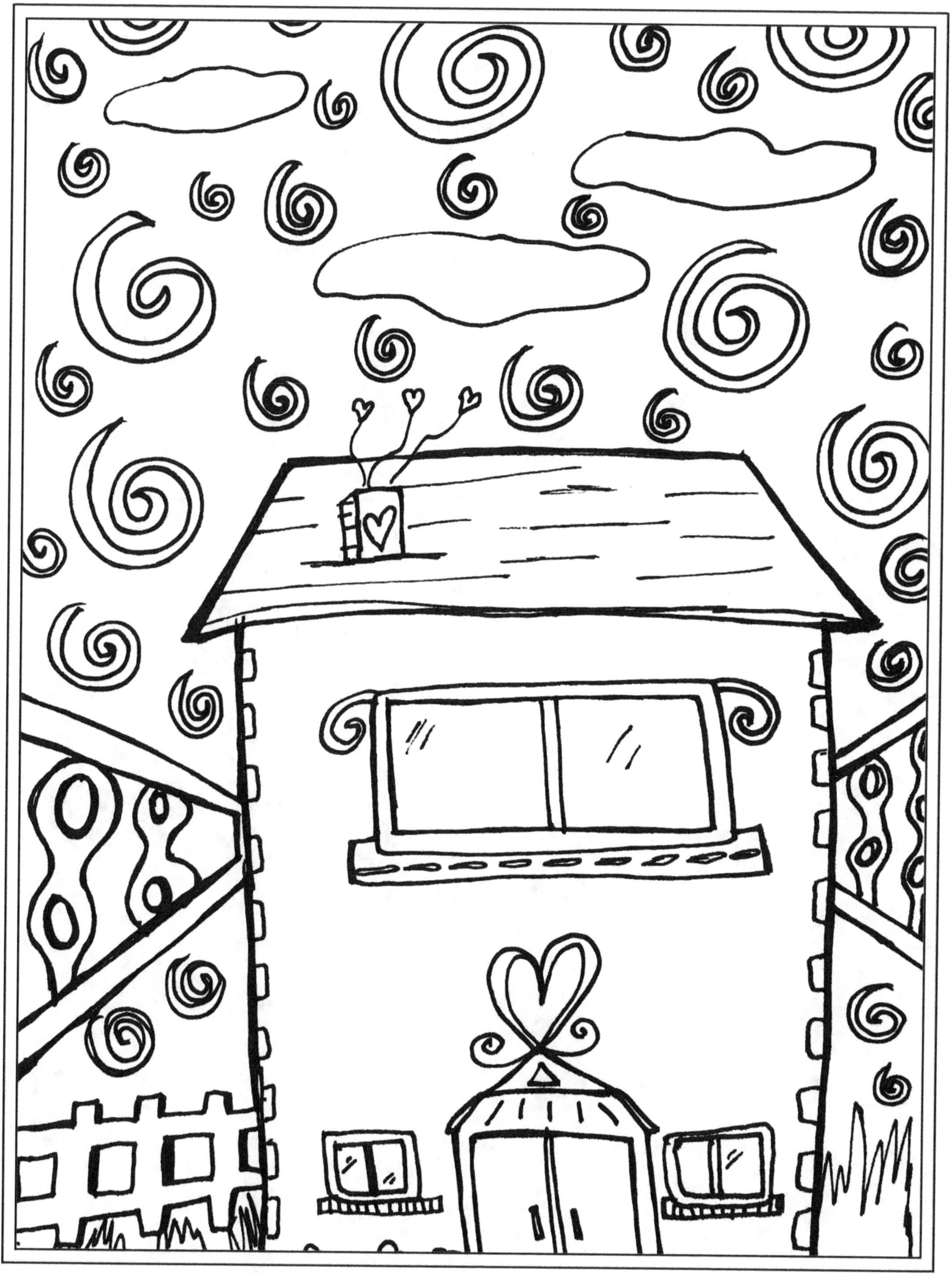

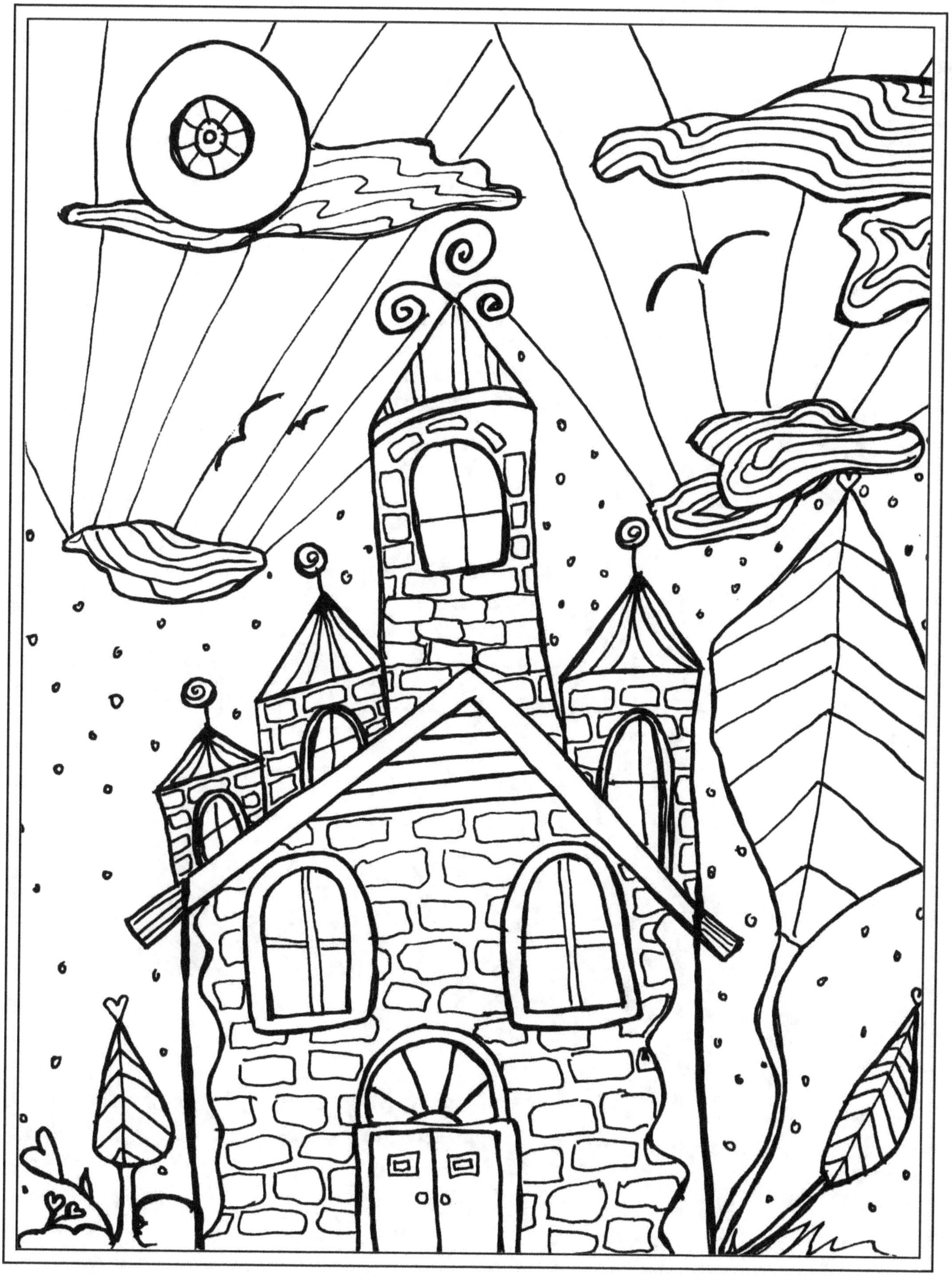

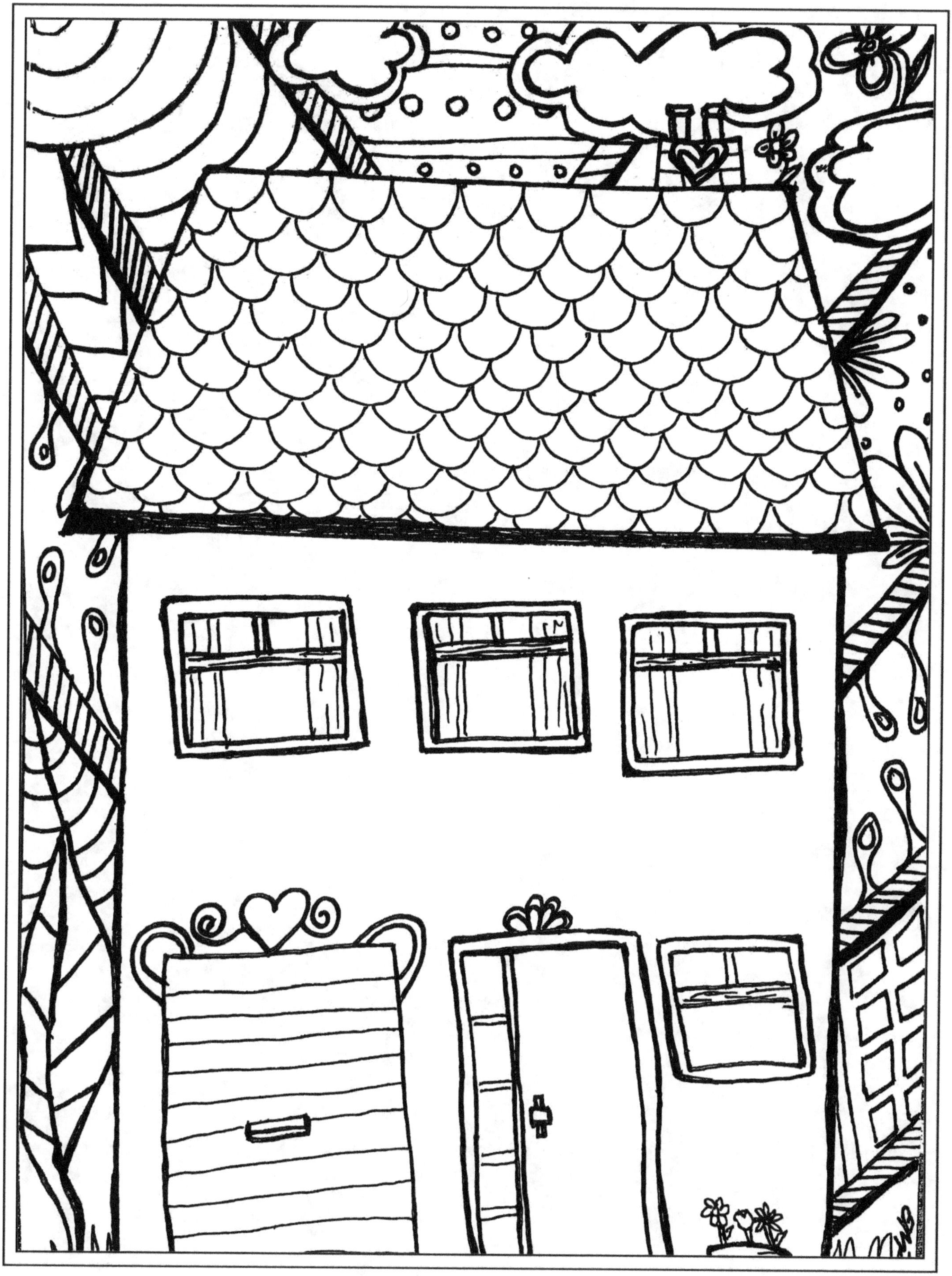

www.ingramcontent.com/pod-product-compliance
Lightning Source LLC
Chambersburg PA
CBHW081125180526
45170CB00008B/3001
9781542385909